Better Homes·and Gardens®

FAST Scrapbooking

Meredith® Books
Des Moines, Iowa

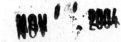

FASTScrapbooking

Editor:	Carol Field Dahlstrom
Designer:	Catherine Brett
Writer and Project Designer:	Susan M. Banker
Contributing Writer and Project Designer:	Janet Petersma
Project Designers:	Linda Franklin, Joan Friedenfels, Connie Lamb, Diane Reams, Cheryl Thieleke, Heather Vinall
Exclusive Paper and Project Designer:	Alice Wetzel
Exclusive Paper Designer and Illustrator:	Sue Cornelison
Technical Assistant:	Judy Bailey
Copy Chief:	Terri Fredrickson
Publishing Operations Manager:	Karen Schirm
Managers, Book Production:	Pam Kvitne, Marjorie J. Schenkelberg, Rick von Holdt, Mark Weaver
Contributing Copy Editor:	Arianna McKinney
Contributing Proofreaders:	Jessica Kearney Heidgerken, Karen Schmidt, Margaret Smith
Photographers:	Meredith Photo Studio
Technical Illustrators:	Shawn Drafahl, Chris Neubauer Graphics, Inc.
Editorial Assistants:	Kaye Chabot, Cheryl Eckert
Edit and Design Production Coordinator:	Mary Lee Gavin

MEREDITH® BOOKS

Editor in Chief:	Linda Raglan Cunningham
Design Director:	Matt Strelecki
Managing Editor:	Gregory H. Kayko
Executive Editor:	Jennifer Dorland Darling

Publisher:	James D. Blume
Executive Director, Marketing:	Jeffrey Myers
Executive Director, New Business Development:	Todd M. Davis
Executive Director, Sales:	Ken Zagor
Director, Operations:	George A. Susral
Director, Production:	Douglas M. Johnston
Business Director:	Jim Leonard

Vice President and General Manager: Douglas J. Guendel

BETTER HOMES AND GARDENS® MAGAZINE
Editor in Chief: Karol DeWulf Nickell

MEREDITH PUBLISHING GROUP
President, Publishing Group: Stephen M. Lacy
Vice President-Publishing Director: Bob Mate

MEREDITH CORPORATION
Chairman and Chief Executive Officer: William T. Kerr

In Memoriam: E. T. Meredith III (1933–2003)

All of us at Meredith® Books are dedicated to providing you with information and ideas to create beautiful and useful projects. We welcome your comments and suggestions. Write to us at: Meredith Books, Crafts Editorial Department, 1716 Locust Street—LN120, Des Moines, IA 50309-3023.

If you would like to purchase any of our crafts, cooking, gardening, home improvement, or home decorating and design books, check wherever quality books are sold. Or visit us at: bhgbooks.com

Permission granted to photocopy exclusive art in this book for personal use only.

make it fast

OK, let's admit it—we talk on the phone while we make dinner, we eat lunch while we drive the kids to piano lessons, and we seldom sit down to watch television unless we're folding clothes at the same time. We drive up to get our food, instant message to talk to our friends, and expect next-day delivery on just about everything. Whether we are overbooked moms, overstressed wives, or overworked employees, everywhere we go we need to make it fast! But we still love to keep track of our day-to-day memories with our favorite thing to do—scrapbooking!

In this book of fast scrapbooking ideas, we've kept your busy life in mind. We've given you tips on how to get (and stay) organized and how to design pages that look like a million but only take a few minutes to create. We've shown you how to use innovative scrapbooking tools that should save you hours and products to make the best use of your valuable time. We've also supplied technique ideas for using eyelets, fiber, kits, tags, vellums, and more. So grab that sandwich, the kids, the dry cleaning, and then scoop up your photos, card stock, and stickers. You'll be surprised how many pages you can create before that next load of laundry is ready to fold!
Happy scrapping!

Carol Field Dahlstrom

Carol Field Dahlstrom, Editor

It's always about the kids

Childrens' lives consist of many highlights, such as embracing an animal, playing a sport, and discovering the world. Capture all the precious times with pages dedicated to the kids.

44

Family fun & play with pets

Gather your greatest family photos—including those starring the family pets! This sentimental chapter offers 16 clever and quick scrapbook page ideas to record your favorite memories in a flash.

82

contents

Places to go, things to do

Whether you call them trips, travels, adventures, vacations, or get-aways, remember all of the fun, can't-wait-to-go-again times on scrapbook pages that are worth a return visit.

102

Preserving memories

Maybe you glow with pride when you see a photo of a loved one in the service. Or perhaps snapshots of the garden make you smile. Place those heartwarming images center-stage.

128

how to use
this book

All in one convenient book—
YOU'LL LEARN:
- which supplies to get and how to use them
- tips to make great-looking pages, plus a glossary to clarify the terminology

YOU'LL GET:
- materials lists and helpful pointers to re-create each sample page
- exclusive papers, headlines, and quotes to make scrapbooking easy

For those new to scrapbooking or those who have been cropping for years, this book reviews the tools, tips, and techniques needed for successful scrapbooking and provides oodles of ideas to make pages fast without sacrificing the look. For a basic review of tools and supplies, check out pages 8–17. Grab some tips from the scrapping experts on pages 18–41. And scour the glossary of scrapbooking terms on pages 148–151 to help you along the way.

Making the Pages

To help you reproduce the 100 timesaving pages in this book, each scrapbook page includes an overview of what makes the page fast to create, a quick tip, a materials list, pointers to guide you through the process, and a drawing that illustrates how to arrange the main layers.

① The Make it Fast Overview

The paragraph at the top of each page gives a brief explanation why the page is quick to create, including use of stickers, color blocking, and photo arrangement.

② The Quick Tips

Circular close-ups highlight a detail from the page and give a tip to make creating the feature quick and easy.

③ The Materials List

The side column includes a complete list of the scrapbooking supplies used to make the page. Starting with photos or other artistic creations, the list continues with papers, embellishments, tools, and adhesives.

④ The Callouts

At the bottom of each page, a line links captions to the related area of the sample scrapbook page to clarify how to construct the page.

emma & honey

make it fast with photo frames. These coordinating frames are
(1) provided on pages 161 and 177. Cut them out and layer them
on additional papers to make the page rich with color.

2 QUICK TIP

Use a loop of gold jumpring to hang a paper tag from ½-inch-wide ribbon.

3

materials

- photos; 12-inch square of green polka-dot paper
- rust subtle-pattern scrapbook paper
- dark green card stock
- color photocopy of mats and tag, pages 161 and 177
- ½-inch-wide gold and burgundy ribbon
- gold jumpring
- paper punch
- paper trimmer
- black marking pen
- crafts knife; glue stick

Art in back of book!

6

see pages 161 and 177

Punch a hole in the top edge of the tag. Thread ribbon through a jumpring; attach the tag.
■
4

Fold ribbon back and forth vertically on the page, adhering in spots with glue stick.
■

Trim a wider green mat to the back provided decorative mat. Cut out the frame center using a crafts knife.
■

5

5 The Drawings

Below the materials list is a black and white drawing to show the arrangement of the major components of the page. Some of the details, such as stickers, are eliminated on the drawing to allow a clearer understanding of the page composition.

6 Art in Back of Book

When you see this circular image, find the corresponding exclusive scrapbooking artwork printed in the back of the book. This section includes frames, borders, and other decorative details to photocopy and use.

And there's more!

Instant Headlines

You'll find several quick headlines at the end of each chapter. To have these headlines on hand, make several photocopies and keep them in a large envelope. Permission is given in the front of the book to photocopy these headlines for personal use.

Quick Journaling

Throughout the book you'll discover dozens of ways to journal. When you're at a loss for what to say, use these tips to find inspiration in a jiffy:

- Use personal or famous quotes (see page 145)
- Use dictionary definitions (see page 57)
- Use preprinted materials, such as newspaper clippings or brochures (see page 125)
- Take notes or keep a journal when taking photographs

gather your supplies

Getting started is half the fun of scrapbooking. Just walk into any scrapbooking store and find yourself wonderfully lost in a paradise of gorgeous papers, intricate die cuts and stickers, punches and stamps of every imaginable shape, a counter full of adhesives, and embellishments pretty enough to wear. The supply options open to scrapbookers are amazing, and that makes the shopping awesome!

Supplies used to make the scrapbook pages in this book are listed below and through page 13. Keep these items on hand to scrapbook whenever your schedule allows. Because the focus of this book is fast scrapbooking, tips are provided so you can spend less time at the store and more time making memorable pages!

Many of the sample scrapbook pages in this book use the following supplies:

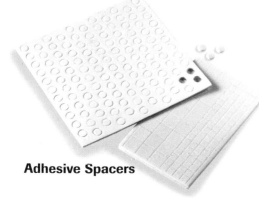

Adhesive Mesh

Adhesive Mesh
This adhesive-backed mesh is plastic and is available in a range of widths and colors. Placed on a scrapbook page, the mesh creates a gridded texture.

Adhesive Spacers

Adhesive Spacers
These adhesives are packaged in rolls or sheets. Varying in size, shape, and thickness, the spacers hold papers together as well as raise a paper layer from the background.

Adhesive Tabs
The purpose of this type of adhesive is mainly to adhere papers, including photos. It comes on a roll in an easy-to-use applicator.

Adhesive Tabs

Alphabet and Word Stickers

Available in a gamut of styles from playful to refined, these stickers give journaling, headlines, and labels a professional look.

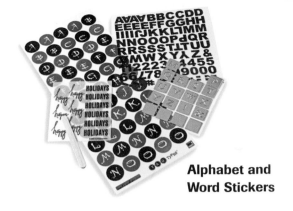

Alphabet and Word Stickers

Brads

Scrapbooking stores offer decorative brads that contribute instant detail to pages. Each brad has two prongs on the back that insert through paper(s) and then bend outward and flat to to secure the paper in place. The mini trims are available in several shapes and colors.

Brads

Corner Scissors

These scissors transform a right-angle corner into a decorative shape. The blades have guides for positioning the paper before cutting. Some brands offer more than one cutting choice, such as the pictured pair of scissors, which features four options.

Corner Scissors

Decorating Chalk

While sidewalk chalk smears or rubs off after application, this type is more permanent. Decorating chalk is available in a rainbow of colors at scrapbooking and stamping stores. Apply it with your finger or the applicator that comes with the chalk.

Decorating Chalk

Decorative-Edge Scissors

Decorative-Edge Scissors

Available in many different styles, decorative-edge scissors enable a scrapbooker to trim paper so it has a repeating pattern on the edge.

Die Cuts

Die Cuts

Die cuts are paper shapes that can be simple or intricate in design. Some purchased die cuts use layering to develop detail to the design. Those shown here have detailed laser cuts to give them a realistic appearance. Or make your own die cuts using punches or templates.

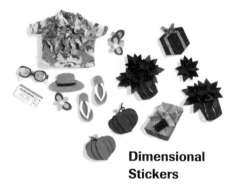

Dimensional Stickers

Dimensional Stickers

These fun theme stickers are miniature representations of the real thing. The adhesive-backed stickers are created from a variety of materials, including fabric, paper, and plastic, and often have such details as beads and glitter.

Double-sided Adhesive

Double-sided Adhesive

Available in the form of tape, several brands are available for scrapbooking. The style shown here is permanent, tacky enough to hold micro beads, and comes in a roll dispenser.

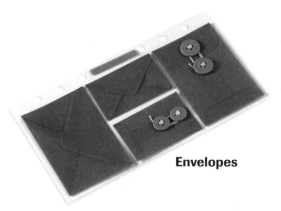

Envelopes

Envelopes

A charming embellishment that works for many scrapbook layouts, envelopes are made in several sizes, colors, and papers. Shown here are small vellum envelopes with traditional flap and button-wrap closures.

Eyelet Tools

Two types of eyelet tools are available. One is a handheld setter that resembles a paper punch. The other type includes an eyelet setter (small metal rod), a protective mat, and a hammer.

Eyelet Setters

Eyelets

Made from thin metal, eyelets are usually pea-size, but larger ones also are available. When used for scrapbooking, they hold papers together, create a hole for threading fiber, or accent a feature of the page.

Eyelets

Fibers

Available in a variety of colors, textures, and lengths, these threads usually are sold as an assortment on cards and are used to enhance scrapbooking pages.

Fibers

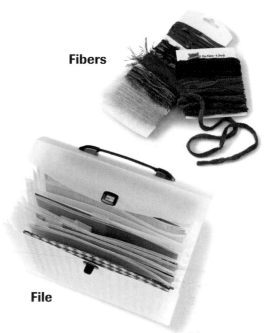

File

A handy accessory for scrapbooking, this case has divided sections to store papers or pages until they are put in an album.

File

Glue Sticks

These adhesives are encased in a tube. Some of this type of glue is temporary, allowing you to reposition the item being glued. Use it along paper edges or in corners.

Glue Sticks

Marking Pens

Available in a rainbow of colors and widths, these pens are used often for journaling or coloring in small details.

Marking Pens

Metal Embellishments

Metal Embellishments

Used to enhance scrapbook pages quickly, metal embellishments include mini frames, trims, charms, chains, and other items. When choosing embellishments, consider the weight and placement of the items.

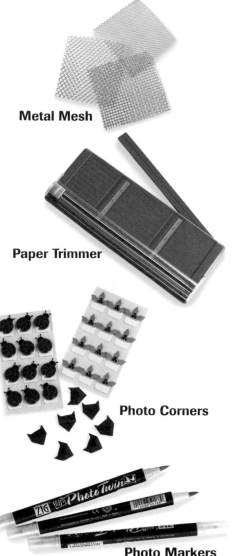

Metal Mesh

Metal Mesh

This mesh is similar to window screen, and available in sheets of different designs and colors.

Paper Trimmer

Paper Trimmer

This is a gridded bed with a blade arm that cuts straight lines in paper. An essential scrapbooking tool, a paper trimmer makes cutting strips, squares, and rectangles quick and easy.

Photo Corners

Photo Corners

For years, photo corners were used to hold photos in albums without placing adhesive directly on the photo back. Scrapbookers now have photo corners with intricate designs to complement the theme of the page.

Photo Markers

Photo Markers

These pastel markers give subtle color to black-and-white photos. The different tip widths allow for coloring in large or small areas.

Precut Papers

Precut Papers

Scrapbooking stores carry a selection of types of papers cut into squares and rectangles to make color-blocking and matting swift and simple. Purchase these papers in a bag or in a stack that is bound on one edge.

Protective Sleeves

Usually acid-free, these plastic pockets come in sizes to fit scrapbooks. The sleeves protect pages from deteriorating elements.

Protective Sleeves

Rubber Stamps and Ink Pad

Transfer images of all sorts to paper using rubber stamps. The raised area on the stamp is pressed onto an ink pad and then pressed onto paper. Thousands of stamp designs are available, and ink pads come in every color, including metallics and blends.

Rubber Stamps and Ink Pad

Scissors

The type of scissors that works best for scrapbooking is sharp, short, and pointed, to enable you to make detail cuts on paper.

Scissors

Tags

Premade tags lend quick detail to scrapbooking pages and can be used as a background for journaling, stickers, labeling, or other embellishments. The tags shown here have metal edges. The punched hole allows for attachment using such items as fibers, brads, or eyelets.

Tags

Vanishing-Ink Pen

This marking pen has ink that fades, perfect for creating a temporary mark or guide.

Vanishing-Ink Pen

how to use
your supplies

Photo Trimmer

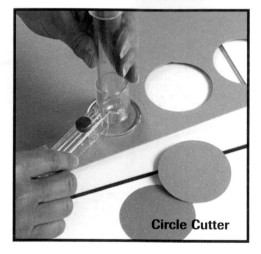

Circle Cutter

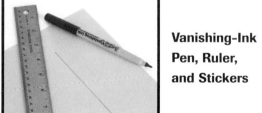

Vanishing-Ink Pen, Ruler, and Stickers

Trimming Photos

A small version of a paper trimmer, this convenient tool has a flat gridded surface for measuring and a blade that makes straight cuts. Some models have a shield next to the blade to hold the photo in place when pressure is applied. Use this tool with caution and keep fingers away from the blade.

To use the trimmer, lift the blade arm up by the handle with one hand. With the other hand, position the photo on the gridded surface, using the lines for measurement. Press on the shield and carefully push the blade handle down until the length of the photo is cut.

Cutting Circles

Cut out perfect circles using this device, which has a sharp blade that follows the shape of the base. Most circle cutters are sold with a mat made specially for protecting the work surface. The cutter shown here comes with a thick square of glass.

To use the cutter, determine the size of circle desired and adjust the blade to that size. Set a protective mat on the cutting surface. Place the paper to be cut on the protective mat. Position the cutter on the paper, apply pressure to the top handle, and move the blade arm around the circular center.

To make half circles, place the tool at the paper edge or cut a whole circle in half with scissors.

Aligning Alphabet Stickers

To draw a rule for perfect alignment, use a vanishing ink pen. This temporary line helps when placing alphabet stickers as well as photos, journaling, and more.

First use a ruler and a vanishing ink pen to draw a line where you want the letters. Use this line as a guide for positioning letters. The line will disappear soon.

Trimming Paper

A paper trimmer has a flat gridded surface for measuring and a blade that makes straight cuts. Available in several sizes and styles, these trimmers make cutting large sheets of paper a breeze. Some models have a shield next to the blade to hold the paper in place when pressure is applied. Use this tool with caution and keep fingers away from the blade.

To use the trimmer, lift the blade arm up by the handle with one hand. With the other hand, position the paper on the gridded surface, using the lines for measurement. Press on the shield and carefully push the blade handle down until the length of the paper is cut.

Paper Trimmer

Securing Brads

A great jazzy way to decorate with small accents of color and shape, these metal embellishments are super-simple to apply to scrapbook pages. Brads are available in round, square, and decorative shapes.

Use a pencil to mark brad placement. Punch a tiny hole at the mark to avoid bending the paper. From the front of the paper, insert the prongs through the hole, separate the prongs, and bend them outward from one another until flat against the back of the paper.

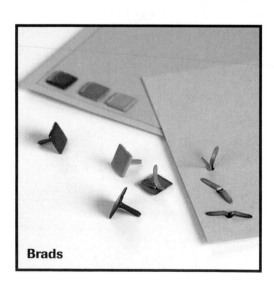

Brads

Handheld Eyelet Tool

Eyelet Tool, Mat, and Hammer

Decorating Chalk

Setting Eyelets

Eyelets are small metal embellishments that leave a hole in the center of the design once set. They hold papers together and serve as design elements. Eyelets are available in a wide assortment of shapes and colors, including metallic.

There are two methods for setting eyelets. For either method, use a pencil to mark the eyelet placement. Punch a tiny hole at the mark and insert the tube part of the eyelet into the hole from the front of the paper.

One method of securing the eyelet is to use a handheld tool, *above left*. Resembling a paper punch, the tool clamps the eyelet, spreading apart the small tube area of the eyelet to hold the paper between the front and back of it. When using this tool, hold it so the tooth (bump) is on the bottom. Insert the tooth into the tube part of the eyelet and squeeze closed. This technique limits the positioning of the eyelet, as it only reaches a short length from the edge of the paper.

The second method is to use an eyelet tool (small metal rod), a protective mat, and a hammer. Place the eyelet through the starter hole and turn, right side down, on the protective mat. Place the eyelet tool in the tube part of the eyelet and strike with a hammer until secure.

Chalking Paper

Available in scrapbooking stores, decorating chalk comes in a plethora of colors to create several effects. Scrapbooking chalk does not rub off or smudge after application. Use it to color elements, such as outlined letters, or to make a shadow around the edge of paper. This technique often is done using brown or black to give a vintage look.

Attaching Micro Beads

Micro beads are sand-size balls that give color, shine, and texture to many surfaces, including paper.

A quick way to create a strip of beaded texture is to place a strip of double-sided tape on paper and pour beads on the tape. Scrapbooking stores carry a selection of tape widths for this purpose. When pouring beads, place the paper in a shallow container to catch the excess beads.

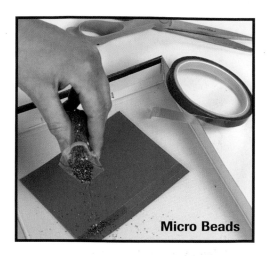

Micro Beads

Using Adhesive Spacers

Adhesive spacers are sticky foam pads sold in dots, squares, and rolls that are tacky on both sides. They quickly attach an element to the background paper, raising it from the page. Spacers are available in a range of sizes and thicknesses.

To use the spacers, remove one side of the backing paper and press onto the element to be attached. Remove the backing paper from the other side of spacer and place the element where desired. Depending on the size of the element, you may want to use more than one spacer.

Adhesive Spacers

Using Templates

Templates (stencils) are plastic or cardboard sheets that have die-cut shapes used for patterns. Most templates have several shapes on one sheet.

To use a template, lay it on the paper to which you wish to transfer the design. Using a pencil, trace around the template. Use the drawn line as a guide for coloring, writing, and cutting.

Templates

Creating Journaling

A quick way to ensure journaling in a straight line is to use the edge of a rectangle of heavy paper, such as card stock.

To use the straightedge, align the edge with the paper to be journaled. Use the edge of the card stock to guide writing. For letters with descenders (letter parts that fall below the guide line), write in descenders when all the journaling is complete. Replace the card stock when the edge becomes indented.

Straightedge Journaling

8 terrific tips!

1 Get organized

Scrapbooking progresses more smoothly when your photos are organized beforehand. Choose only the best photos to represent each event.

2 Set aside time

The most productive scrapbookers regularly set aside time to work on their albums. Whether it's late at night after the kids are in bed or a weekend evening spent cropping, schedule time for scrapbooking.

3 Do your prework

Break your scrapbooking into smaller tasks to do at opportune times. Perhaps make a bag of punched shapes while waiting to pick up a child from dance or cut paper strips while watching TV.

4 Have a goal for each page

Think about the main point of the page. What message are you trying to convey?

⑤ Copy pages you like

Whether it's an original sketch or an idea from a book or magazine, use these layouts as models for your pages.

⑥ Repeat, repeat, repeat

When you find a layout you like, repeat it on another scrapbook page later in your album using different colors and embellishments. If possible, make the pages during one sitting for efficiency.

⑦ Shop with photos in hand

Select photos, put them in an envelope, and take them with you when shopping at the scrapbook store. Pick out papers and embellishments to coordinate with the photos, asking for assistance from the store staff if needed.

⑧ Make a theme album

Choose the same color scheme and embellishments for an entire album to create continuity in the album's look and feel. This works well for many types of themes, such as baby and wedding. It also saves time selecting items for each page.

10 timesaving actions

1 Mix Print Paper and Card Stock

Use strips of card stock and print paper in varying widths to construct your layout in no time. Use premade strips or cut or tear your own. (See an example on *page 22.*)

2 Use a Page Kit

A nicely designed page kit yields layouts in a flash. Choose a kit carefully; look for colors that coordinate with your photos. Often page kits contain enough materials to complete several pages. (See an example on *page 24.*)

3 Use a Monochromatic Color Scheme

Planning appropriate colors for scrapbook pages is often difficult and time-consuming. One way to speed up the process is to use a monochromatic (one-color) theme. Choose a focus color; then choose coordinating card stock in at least three shades of that color—light, medium, and dark. (See an example on *page 26.*)

4 Mat with Premade Frames

Use premade frames to save work. The frames, often accompanied by matching embellishments, fill your pages and give a professional look instantly. Choose your frames carefully to match photos and papers. (See an example on *page 28.*)

5 Color-Block the Background

Color-blocking is a simple technique in which blocks of solid or print card stock or papers are arranged to create a background or photo mat. Select three to four colors from your photos and choose papers to match. (See an example on *page 30.*)

6 Create a Title from Stickers

Use alphabet stickers to create a headline block, selecting stickers that complement the theme. Press them on card stock, leaving room for journaling if desired. Embellish the page with coordinating decorative stickers. (See an example on *page 32.*)

7 Rubber-Stamp the Background

Customize a layout with rubber stamps by stamping randomly on the background paper. Use acid-free scrapbooking ink that coordinates with layout colors. To make embellishments, stamp on a piece of card stock and cut around the shapes for an economic alternative to stickers. (See an example on *page 34.*)

8 Create a Large Vertical Headline

Divide your layout into imaginary thirds. Print or place your headline on a strip of card stock to cover the left third of the page. Fill the remainder of the page with evenly spaced photos. (See an example on *page 36.*)

9 Make Borders from Punches

Punches are available in a wide range of designs and sizes to create instant borders. Punch shapes from paper scraps and align them to that make thrifty substitutes purchased borders. (See an example on *page 38.*)

10 Make a Single-Photo Layout

Choose a good photo and let it do most of the work. If the photo image is strong or enlarged, little embellishment is needed. (See an example on *page 40.*)

For examples using these timesaving actions, see *pages 22–41.*

SWEET HEARTS

Ever since she started school, Bailey has made her Valentines. Sometimes her projects get a bit complicated (like the year she made little airplanes out of sticks of gum), and her 4th grade year was no exception. We found an idea in *Family Fun* magazine to cut Rice Krispie bars out with a heart-shaped cookie cutter. Since Bailey had won a first place prize for her Rice Krispie bars at the fair, she thought this would be a great plan. The only problem was that we had to make multiple pans of bars in order to cut out all the hearts! Then of course we had to eat all of the scraps. The finished products were sprinkled with colorful decorations and packaged in clear bags. She was pleased with how they turned out!

February, 2002 – Age 9

1 mix print paper and card stock

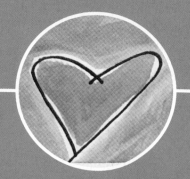

make it quick by mixing strips of scrapbook paper and card stock as the starting point for an effective design. Buy premade strips or cut your own. This technique is a handy way to use up leftover paper and rations your paper over multiple pages. This example combines strips of each in varying widths.

more quick tips for making this page

1. Choose a print paper to coordinate with your photos.

2. Choose two or three colors of card stock to go with the print paper.

3. Tear a wide strip of print paper for the left side. Back it with two narrow strips of card stock. This serves to separate visually the print paper from the other colors in the layout.

4. Use a very wide block of one color on the bottom half of the layout.

5. Buy two-tone card stock (a different color on each side) to simplify paper selection and multiply options.

6. Cut an element from print paper to make an embellishment.

7. Use a die-cut machine to customize a coordinating headline.

8. Apply punched dots at the top of each die-cut letter.

Hoppy

Easter

EGGS

Bailey enjoys making creative designs on her Easter eggs, carefully dipping and examining each one to be sure it is just right!

Bailey, Age 9 March, 2002.

Coloring Eggs

2 use a page kit

make it quick with scrapbooking kits that are available in a wide range of themes. Put together layouts in a flash with a nicely designed page kit that provides coordinating headlines, corners, die cuts, embellishments, mats, and journal boxes. If you wish, customize your page by incorporating your own supplies.

more quick tips for making this page

1. Split the color of the background.

2. Contribute elements that correspond to the premade items, such as the torn strip of yellow layered on orange at the page bottom.

3. Print journaling on vellum and mat on the box provided, or write directly on the journal box.

4. Print journaling and punch out a circle to make a tag; embellish with fiber.

5. Use the corners from the kit to frame the page.

SEA ISLAND

Old-world grandeur and natural beauty

view of surrounding marshes

The Cloister

Sea Island mansions

June 9, 2003

After dinner at a Mediterranean restaurant on St. Simons Island (where Jan enjoyed crab cakes again), we drove across the bridge to Sea Island. We had heard about it, as Jay's great uncle Curt is a frequent golfing guest at the world-class hotel, The Cloister. Since 1928, Sea Island has been the domain of The Cloister hotel. Today, in addition to the hotel, it is home to some of the most elegant villas and mansions in the Southeast. The island is an exclusively residential with no businesses. Most of Sea Island's homes--many in the Spanish-Mediterranean style--are second homes to wealthy families and executives. The island was originally acquired by Ohio-based Howard Earle Coffin, an automobile executive, in 1925. Still owned by Coffin's descendants, The Cloister combines 10,000 acres of forest, lawn, and marshland, plus 5 miles of beachfront. Dignitaries from around the world have been guests at The Cloister, including Margaret Thatcher, Queen Juliana of the Netherlands, and four U.S. presidents.

As much as we had read about Sea Island, however, we were unprepared for the astounding natural splendor of the island, a heavily wooded area with beautifully manicured properties. In addition to The Cloister, these photos show two of the breathtaking mansions we saw along the one street that runs the length of Sea Island. Tropical foliage and blue hydrangeas graced many lawns. Jay and Jan could imagine how it might feel to live in this fabulous setting, but the idea didn't appeal to Bailey!

3 monochromatic
color scheme

make it quick by choosing a single color scheme. Base the focus color on the main color in your photos; then choose coordinating card stock in at least three shades of that color—light, medium, and dark.

more quick tips for making this page

1. Choose three shades of the main color. Use the darker colors for the background and the lightest for the headline and journaling.

2. Use a basic color-block design.

3. Mat a photo as part of the headline design.

4. Use only card stock, adhering punched dots to highlight journaling.

5. Cut a piece of the medium color in half lengthwise; then place part of it on each page as the layout center color.

6. Print journaling and headline on light card stock and mount.

7. Leave all photos unmatted except the one on the headline strip.

8. Punch squares to dress up a card stock block.

On Her Way

④

①

⑤

③
My mom felt strongly that Bailey needed rollerblades so she could learn to skate like the other kids. Bailey is not a particularly athletic child, and I resisted, worried that she might fall and get hurt. Sure enough, rollerblades showed up at Christmas from Grandma and Grandpa, and Bailey could not wait for a warm enough day to try them out. I was still mightily skeptical. Thinking about her on rollerblades made a knot in my stomach.

That mild February day, Bailey pulled on the rollerblades and tied them tightly. Afraid to skate down the gentle slope of the driveway, she walked through the grass all the way to the sidewalk. Then surprisingly, away she rolled. Not fast, but steady. Not falling down, but standing tall.

When I look back on this moment, I recall my natural tendency to want to protect and shelter this little girl. But watching her, I see how she can fly, if I just have the confidence and faith to let her go.

②

⑥

Feb '02
Age 9

4 mat with premade frames

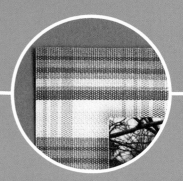

make it quick using premade frames to immediately give a professional look to your page. Scrapbooking stores carry a variety of frames, including solids, prints, and themes. Frame sets make for even easier scrapbooking. If the frame cutout is too small, a quick solution is to mount the photo on top.

more quick tips for making this page

1. Coordinate the background paper with the frame and photos.

2. Split the background into two colors for enhanced interest and place a strip of contrasting paper at the bottom of the page.

3. Print journaling, leaving space for a headline.

4. Print your headline in matching ink or use alphabet stickers. Mat in coordinating colors.

5. Accent with color strips to separate the headline space from the journaling and to draw the eye to the bottom of the page.

6. Mat the primary photo with a precut frame.

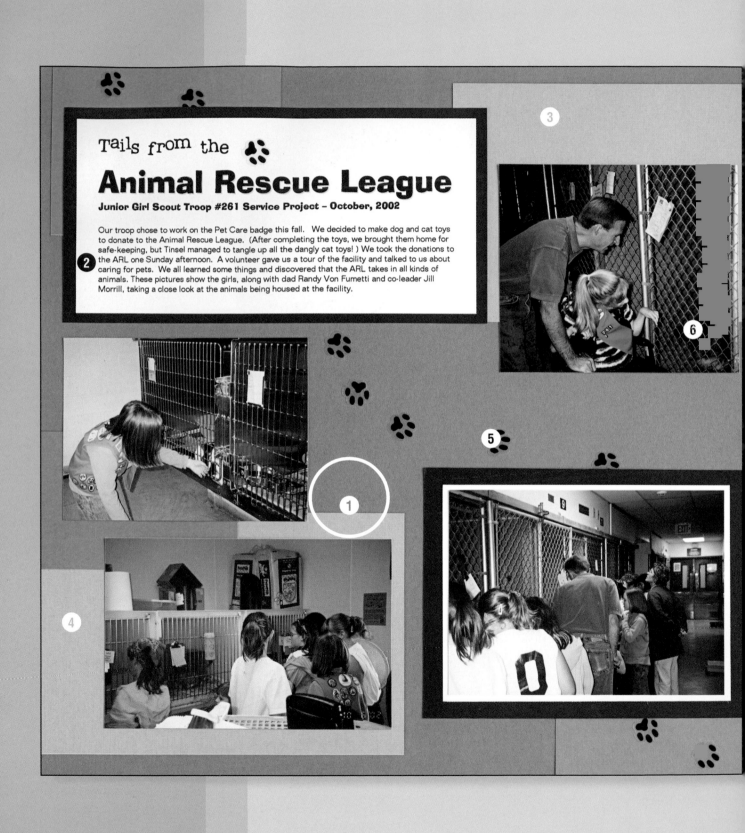

Tails from the
Animal Rescue League
Junior Girl Scout Troop #261 Service Project – October, 2002

Our troop chose to work on the Pet Care badge this fall. We decided to make dog and cat toys to donate to the Animal Rescue League. (After completing the toys, we brought them home for safe-keeping, but Tinsel managed to tangle up all the dangly cat toys!) We took the donations to the ARL one Sunday afternoon. A volunteer gave us a tour of the facility and talked to us about caring for pets. We all learned some things and discovered that the ARL takes in all kinds of animals. These pictures show the girls, along with dad Randy Von Fumetti and co-leader Jill Morrill, taking a close look at the animals being housed at the facility.

5 color-block
the background

make it quick using a simple technique in which blocks of solid or print card stock or paper are placed in a random pattern to create a background or photo mat. Arrange the blocks of color around your page to create an interesting background that perfectly coordinates with the photos.

more quick tips for making this page

1 Select three to four colors from the photos and choose paper and card stock to match those colors.

2 Print the headline and journaling on a light color.

3 Cut or tear rectangles and squares from the remaining colors in varying sizes.

4 Balance the colors and shapes on the layout.

5 Place coordinating stickers diagonally on the page to quickly add movement to the page.

6 Allow the color blocks to back most of the photos.

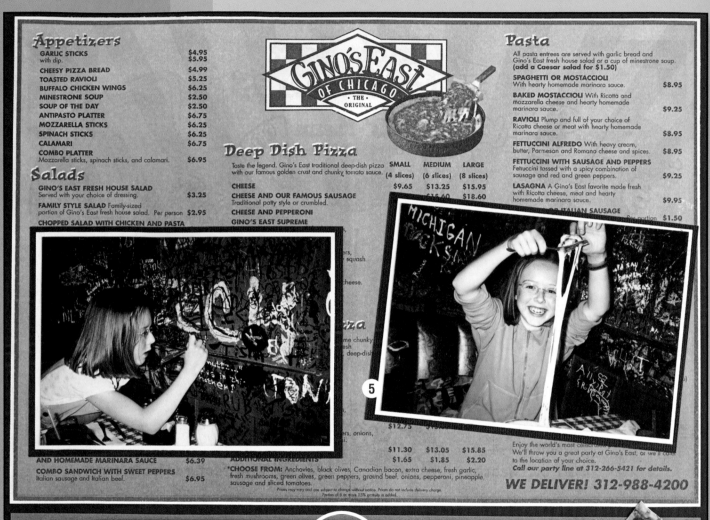

Appetizers

GARLIC STICKS	$4.95
with dip.	$5.95
CHEESY PIZZA BREAD	$4.99
TOASTED RAVIOLI	$5.25
BUFFALO CHICKEN WINGS	$6.25
MINESTRONE SOUP	$2.50
SOUP OF THE DAY	$2.50
ANTIPASTO PLATTER	$6.75
MOZZARELLA STICKS	$6.25
SPINACH STICKS	$6.25
CALAMARI	$6.75
COMBO PLATTER	
Mozzarella sticks, spinach sticks, and calamari.	$6.95

Salads

GINO'S EAST FRESH HOUSE SALAD
Served with your choice of dressing. $3.25

FAMILY STYLE SALAD Family-sized
portion of Gino's East fresh house salad. Per person $2.95

CHOPPED SALAD WITH CHICKEN AND PASTA

GINO'S EAST OF CHICAGO · THE ORIGINAL ·

Deep Dish Pizza

Taste the legend. Gino's East traditional deep-dish pizza with our famous golden crust and chunky tomato sauce.

	SMALL (4 slices)	MEDIUM (6 slices)	LARGE (8 slices)
CHEESE	$9.65	$13.25	$15.95
CHEESE AND OUR FAMOUS SAUSAGE		$15.60	$18.60
Traditional patty style or crumbled.			
CHEESE AND PEPPERONI			
GINO'S EAST SUPREME			

Pasta

All pasta entrees are served with garlic bread and Gino's East fresh house salad or a cup of minestrone soup.
(add a Caesar salad for $1.50)

SPAGHETTI OR MOSTACCIOLI
With hearty homemade marinara sauce. $8.95

BAKED MOSTACCIOLI With Ricotta and mozzarella cheese and hearty homemade marinara sauce. $9.25

RAVIOLI Plump and full of your choice of Ricotta cheese or meat with hearty homemade marinara sauce. $8.95

FETTUCCINI ALFREDO With heavy cream, butter, Parmesan and Romano cheese and spices. $8.95

FETTUCCINI WITH SAUSAGE AND PEPPERS
Fettuccini tossed with a spicy combination of sausage and red and green peppers. $9.25

LASAGNA A Gino's East favorite made fresh with Ricotta cheese, meat and hearty homemade marinara sauce. $9.95

... ITALIAN SAUSAGE ... per portion $1.50

AND HOMEMADE MARINARA SAUCE $6.39

COMBO SANDWICH WITH SWEET PEPPERS
Italian sausage and Italian beef. $6.95

| $11.30 | $13.05 | $15.85 |
| $1.65 | $1.85 | $2.20 |

ADDITIONAL INGREDIENTS
*CHOOSE FROM: Anchovies, black olives, Canadian bacon, extra cheese, fresh garlic, fresh mushrooms, green olives, green peppers, ground beef, onions, pepperoni, pineapple, sausage and sliced tomatoes.

Prices may vary and are subject to change without notice. Prices do not include delivery charge.
Parties of 6 or more 15% gratuity is added.

Enjoy the world's most celebrated ... We'll throw you a great party at Gino's East, or we'll ... to the location of your choice.
Call our party line at 312-266-5421 for details.

WE DELIVER! 312-988-4200

June 28, 2002

Iowa Girl Tries Chicago-Style Pizza at GINO'S

Chicago, IL – Johnston residents Jay and Janet Petersma spent the weekend visiting friends in the Chicago area, where they lived several years ago. Jay and Janet have fond memories of deep-dish Chicago-style pizza, and they were anxious for their daughter, Bailey (9) to try it. "Who wouldn't love this legendary pizza?" Jay asked.

"I'm not sure about this," worried Bailey outside Gino's East. She examined all of the pizza pans hanging around the entrance, then noticed the extensive writing all over the dark walls of the famed restaurant.

Inside, Bailey was only too happy to write her name on the wall near the family's table, something she never would have considered doing at home. Her parents took charge of ordering, and when the pizza came, it was just as good as they remembered it.

"Worth the drive from Johnston," announced Janet.

"Too cheesy," proclaimed Bailey, and promptly put down her fork. For her, this legend was highly over-rated.

6 create a title from stickers

make it quick with alphabet stickers to make an instant headline. Place the stickers on the background paper, the journal box, or, to change the look, place only some of the letters on card stock as shown at left.

more quick tips for making this page

1. Whip up an artistic headline by placing a couple of the alphabet stickers on small card stock rectangles.

2. Use the space at the bottom of the page for journaling. Type the journaling, leaving space for an alphabet sticker headline.

3. Embellish the page with decorative stickers that carry out the theme.

4. Tear and chalk the bottom of the journal block.

5. Mat photos to separate them from the print background.

6. Use a square punch and brads for straightforward page accents.

①

④

Camping at Thomas Mitchell Park

③

②

⑤

⑥

June 28-30, 2001 | Bailey – Age 8
Grandma and Grandpa Keith and Vava were only too happy to steal Bailey away for a short camping trip to Thomas Mitchell Park in Mitchellville. The weather was beautiful and they enjoyed being outdoors. Of course, camping with Grandma and Grandpa isn't really roughing it...their camper has all the comforts of home (and more!) On this trip, they took winding walks through the woods, enjoying the flowers and scurrying animals. At the end of the wooded path is a pond where Bailey fed a group of rather aggressive ducks. They also waded in the creek, where Bailey picked up a stick which she has kept to this day. (Incidentally, this is the same creek where I waded as a child more than 35 years ago!) She was fascinated by all the butterflies hovering around the creek, a few of which landed on her hand, much to her delight. This was a special time for Grandma, Grandpa, and Bailey to spend together. I am very thankful for their close relationship.

7 rubber-stamp
the background

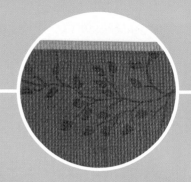

make it quick by using rubber stamps to create a subtle or contrasting pattern in the background. Change the color of the ink to connect an endless array of designs. Choose a rubber stamp and ink color to complement your layout theme. To make die cuts, stamp card stock and trim around the stamp shape.

more quick tips for making this page

1. Stamp a background paper with slightly darker ink for a subtle design.

2. For a spread, cut a sheet of card stock in half and place the halves to appear as mirror images.

3. Print the headline and journaling on vellum to allow the background colors to show through.

4. Mat only the photo that is placed above the headline.

5. Wrap card stock blocks with fiber; tape the ends to the back of the card stock.

6. Use eyelets to attach vellum and to accent the page.

Fall is in the air

Our locust trees have finally grown big enough that we have a few leaves to rake in addition to the pods. While not Jay's favorite activity, having a few leaves to jump in made the task of fall clean-up much more fun for Bailey (age 9), especially when she discovered she could actually fit into the compost bag!

NOV 2 9 2002

8 create a large
vertical headline

make it quick by placing a wide headline strip down the left side to create instant drama. In this example the title is printed directly on a sheet of card stock. Readability is enhanced if the headline reads from bottom to top rather than stacking letters on top of each other.

more quick tips for making this page

1. Mat headline block to extend the full length of the page.

2. Divide the remaining space into two colors to coordinate with the photos.

3. Mat only one photo to create a focal point.

4. Align photos on the page, positioning a strip of coordinating card stock to balance if needed.

5. Use limited embellishments, specifically chosen for color and design, to enhance the layout.

6. Use wider line spacing to improve readability and to fill entire journaling space.

7. Add a date stamp to chronicle the moment.

The Field Museum

Chicago | June 29, 2002

No trip to Chicago would be complete without a visit to this world-famous museum. It had been several years since Jay and Jan had toured it and we were again amazed by the number and diversity of exhibits. Since it was Bailey's first time in such a museum, we wanted her to have an overview of all of it. We wandered through ancient Egypt and Africa and examined everything from prairie plants to precious gems. We checked out the Underground Adventure, where we explored what life is like through the eyes of a bug. (Bailey and Jan fit nicely inside these ant models, but Bailey decided there were way too many creepy crawly critters below ground for her taste!) The highlight of our visit was seeing Sue, the world's largest, most complete, and most famous *tyrannosaurus rex*. It is pretty amazing to think she once walked the face of the earth.

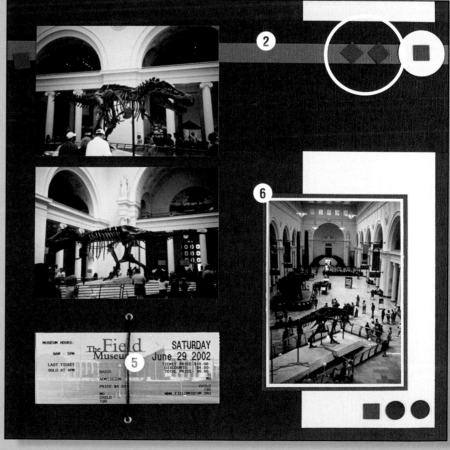

9 make borders from punches

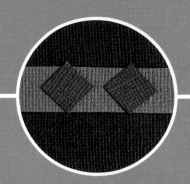

make it quick using punches and paper scraps. Punches are often overlooked in favor of more trendy tools and embellishments. But punches, especially simple geometric shapes, enable you to create simple, timeless designs in no time flat. In this layout, a combination of circle and square punches lends stylish flair.

more quick tips for making this page

1. Print headline and journaling on a large piece of card stock that doubles as a photo mat.

2. Choose four colors of card stock to complement photos. Use these to create strips, borders, and punched pieces.

3. Secure journaling to layout with eyelets.

4. Punch a variety of circles and squares and arrange along the border strips of each page.

5. Memorabilia that may contain acid should be kept away from photos.

6. Mat only the two principal photos.

The heart hath its own memory, like the mind,
and in it are enshrined the precious keepsakes.
-Henry Wadsworth Longfellow

Jekyll Island, Georgia | June, 2003

10 make a single-photo layout

make it quick with a single-photo layout that allows you to explore the deeper meaning of your memories. This serene layout gives you an opportunity to include a special poem, quotation, or journaling to convey your thoughts. This layout features strong lines and monochromatic color so the photo and journaling remain prominent.

1. Select a special photo to mat or frame.

2. Insert an eyelet in one corner of the frame.

3. Print journaling, ragged left, in the appropriate position on a 9×8½-inch card stock rectangle. Mount this piece in the upper right corner of a 12-inch square of darker card stock.

4. Adhere coordinating card stock strips to the background, leaving narrow borders.

5. Embellish the page with punched squares, offsetting their placement for balance.

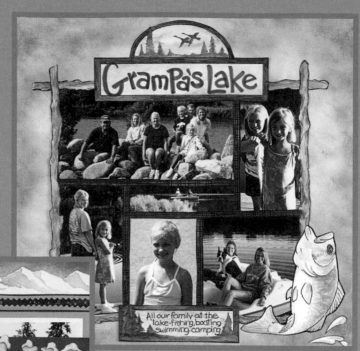

Grampa's Lake

All our family at the
lake-fishing, boating,
swimming, camping

IDAHO

Dearest Friends
Ron and Juanita
Lil and Julian
Donnie and Nancy
and Lori

I love my cat

kitty kitty kitty

Purr MEOW

Anne Mae and Tinker

Madison
age 2

Now that you've learned about scrapbooking tools and techniques, it's time to put your knowledge and creativity to work making pages to cherish for a lifetime.

Inspiring page ideas

Gather those most
treasured photos of
your adorable,
precious, fun-loving,
darling, sweet,
cute-as-a-bug,
smiling, active, gutsy
kids and get ready
to scrap!

It's always
about the kids

Lightly rub sandpaper across blank paper surface to create a distressed look.

materials

- photos
- 12-inch squares of card stock in blue and dark red
- 10½-inch square of blue typed-word print paper
- 11½×2-inch strip of blue and black plaid paper
- 2 brads
- gold buckle
- black alphabet stickers
- "daddy's boy" dimensional stickers
- fine sandpaper
- paper punch
- permanent fine-line black marking pen
- glue stick
- hot-glue gun and glue sticks

daddy's boy

make it fast using three quality close-up photographs and simple embellishments. Choose papers that contrast with the photographs so your baby's face remains the focus on the page.

Create the look of hand-stitched lines using a marking pen.

Balance the red paper strip with a 2-inch-wide plaid paper strip.

Apply alphabet stickers in a wavy line.

Thread the paper strip through the buckle; secure buckle with hot glue.

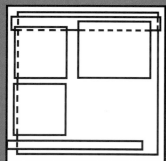

start in art

make it fast with your child's artwork as the main ingredient of the page. Focus attention on the artwork by using a minimum of embellishments.

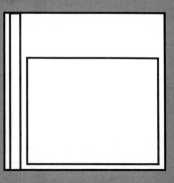

materials
- child's flat artwork
- 12-inch square of light blue card stock
- dark blue card stock
- art-theme border
- alphabet rubber stamp
- black ink pad
- alphabet punch
- paper cutter
- glue stick

CHRISTOPHER'S START IN ART

Place the border vertically on the page.

Mount the artwork on contrasting card stock.

Punch some of the headline letters from the contrasting card stock.

If you don't have the right color of paper on hand, use a piece of fabric.

who's that baby?

make it fast using paper scraps to make a geometric design. Display precut glass and mirrors to carry out the theme and reflect a beautifully artistic image.

materials

- photo
- 12-inch square of blue-gray card stock
- white fiber paper
- iridescent blue paper
- vellum
- black moiré fabric
- large and small silver brads
- small glass and mirror squares and rectangles
- computer and printer
- paper trimmer
- paper punch
- glass adhesive, such as Diamond Glaze Glue
- glue stick

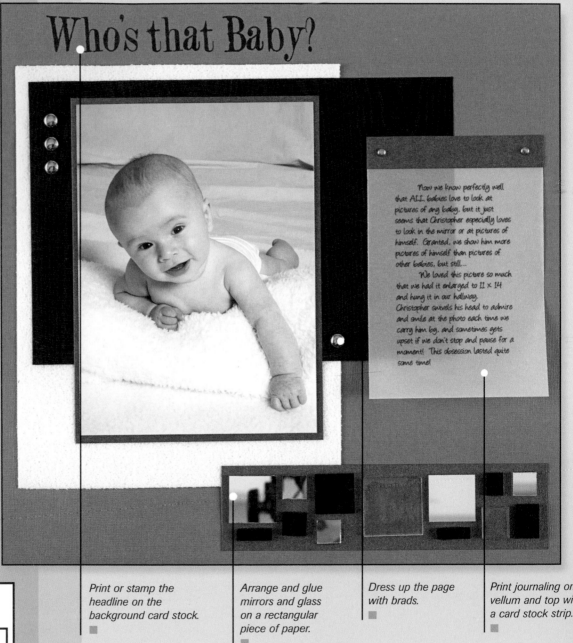

Who's that Baby?

Now we know perfectly well that ALL babies love to look at pictures of any baby, but it just seems that Christopher especially loves to look in the mirror or at pictures of himself. Granted, we show him more pictures of himself than pictures of other babies, but still...

We loved this picture so much that we had it enlarged to 11 × 14 and hung it in our hallway. Christopher swivels his head to admire and smile at the photo each time we carry him by, and sometimes gets upset if we don't stop and pause for a moment! This obsession lasted quite some time!

Print or stamp the headline on the background card stock.

Arrange and glue mirrors and glass on a rectangular piece of paper.

Dress up the page with brads.

Print journaling on vellum and top with a card stock strip.

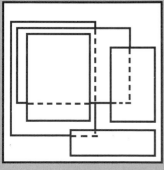

batter up

make it fast using papers and premade embellishments that relate to the photos. Here striped paper imitates the look of the fence, and easy-mount tiles give the impression of a baseball diamond.

"I might be in the Baseball Hall of Fame someday. I know I will be. 'Cause I'm a great slugger."

July 22, 2003

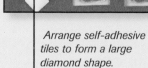

materials

- photos
- 12-inch square of light green card stock
- card stock in light and dark green
- striped gray scrapbook paper
- alphabet stickers
- square punch
- light green self-adhesive tiles
- paper trimmer
- computer and printer
- glue stick

Arrange self-adhesive tiles to form a large diamond shape.

Punch squares in a card stock strip; adhere alphabet stickers in the openings.

Print and mount a quote, leaving room for embellishments at the bottom.

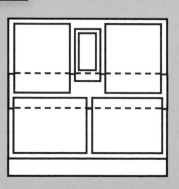

49

firsts

make it fast by framing an enlarged photo with premade art embellishments. These sweet-as-pie headlines, checked border strips, stars, flowers, bugs, and journal boxes are provided on pages 163 and 165.

materials

- photo
- 12-inch square of purple scrapbook paper
- 12-inch square of light yellow orange scrapbook paper
- 12-inch square of polka-dot paper
- color photocopy of art elements, pages 163 and 165
- marking pens in purple and blue
- scissors
- glue stick

Art in back of book!

see page 163

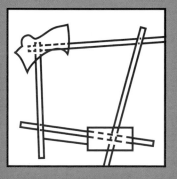

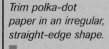

Mount the silhouette on polka-dot paper.

Trim polka-dot paper in an irregular, straight-edge shape.

Cross the border strips at the corners.

QUICK TIP

Salvage a photo with an undesirable background by cropping it and mounting it on paper.

Trim checked strips to make square corners.

Position dots from the bug to the conversation bubble.

Write a comical blurb with a marker.

Art in back of book!

see page 165

Bring attention to the headline by adding a dimensional element.

simply beautiful

make it fast using three shades of one color. To texturize the page, overlay printed vellum, a length of fiber, headline and journal boxes, and a metal heart and frame.

materials

- photos
- 12-inch square of dark pink card stock
- card stock scraps in medium and light pink
- 12-inch square of light pink printed vellum
- metal heart and small photo frame
- computer and printer
- paper trimmer
- thick white crafts glue
- glue stick

Simply Beautiful

Jana Nicole
September 11, 1981
7lbs. 2 ozs.   19 3/4"
Born at 1:35am – Mercy Hospital

Tear pieces of vellum and layer on the page.

Print the headline and tear the edges.

Adhere a length of fiber along the right edge; tape on back.

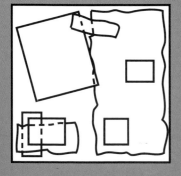

texas princess

make it fast by placing print paper strips above and below a row of mounted photos. Make the strips the same size, allowing room for the photos in the center. Cut the strips slightly smaller than the background paper width to leave a narrow border all around.

Madison

Elaine

Miller

TEXAS PRINCESS ✳ Madison Elaine Miller ✳ TEXAS PRINCESS

materials

- 4 photos, approximately 2½×3½ inches
- 12-inch square of light pink card stock
- 12-inch square of print scrapbook paper
- dark pink card stock
- acetate
- ¼-inch pink grosgrain ribbon
- ⅛-inch pink satin ribbon
- ribbon holders
- metal-edge white tags in two sizes
- flower die cuts in pink and white
- light green marker
- small paper punch
- brads; paper trimmer
- repositionable adhesive; glue stick

Use a brad to hold each flower die cut in place.

Print words on ribbon, using repositionable adhesive to hold ribbon to paper while printing from a computer.

Cut bands of card stock to top each mounted photo.

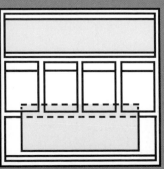

53

Note: gray area indicates top acetate sheet.

first swim

make it fast by coordinating a geometric print background and matting paper. The paper's design enhances the page with instant detail.

materials
- photos
- 12-inch square of geometric print card stock
- coordinating stripe paper for mat
- water-print paper
- white card stock
- white corrugated paper
- chalk in turquoise and green
- glass mosaic tiles in two sizes
- paper cutter
- scissors
- computer and printer
- double-sided tape
- glue stick

Use double-sided tape to hold mosaic tiles in place.

Allow the print in the paper to organize the page.

Choose an outline font to print on patterned scrapbook paper for the headline.

Christopher's

the first ti

Dress up a journal box with corrugated paper and chalk.

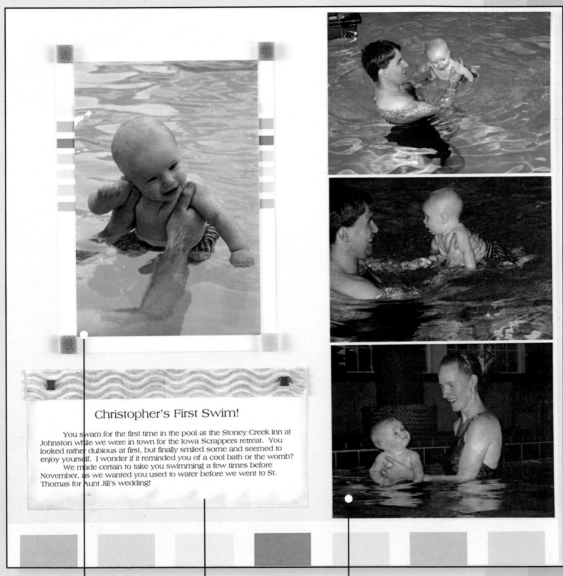

Christopher's First Swim!

You swam for the first time in the pool at the Stoney Creek Inn at Johnston while we were in town for the Iowa Scrappers retreat. You looked rather dubious at first, but finally smiled some and seemed to enjoy yourself. I wonder if it reminded you of a cool bath or the womb?
We made certain to take you swimming a few times before November, as we wanted you used to water before we went to St. Thomas for Aunt Jill's wedding!

Mat a favorite photo as a focal point.

Rub chalk on raised areas of the corrugated strip and on the edges of the journal box.

Align photos vertically, leaving a small space between them.

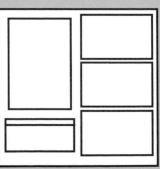

Use a long length of embroidery floss and a sewing needle to make threading buttons easy.

li'l sister big sister

make it fast by mounting one large photo on solid card stock that coordinates with the background paper. Although you could emulate the look of striped background paper, purchase it that way and save yourself time.

materials

- photos
- 12-inch square of partially striped paper
- 3 colors of coordinating card stock
- coordinating small-stripe paper
- coordinating buttons
- white embroidery floss
- sewing needle
- computer and printer
- paper trimmer
- thick white crafts glue
- glue stick

Little sister
Looking up to
Big sister

Jill — 4 yrs.
Jana — 1 mo.
October '87

Organize threaded buttons in rows and adhere with crafts glue.

Choose card stock to stand out from print background paper.

Print headline in three lines to fill space.

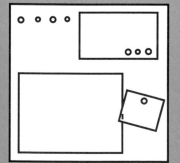

cherish

make it fast by enlarging a favorite photo to 8×10 inches for impact. Overlap it with a word-print paper turned so the words run sideways to prevent detracting from the photo.

WONDER

dream

discover

inspire

Cherish

JOY

fun

cherish (cher´ish) 1. to hold dear; treasure 2. to care for; treat with great care

Use brads to attach the labels.

Print a meaningful word and dictionary definition for the headline.

Glue card stock circles to tags and apply word stickers. Raise the top tag with adhesive spacers.

materials

- 8×10-inch photo
- 12-inch square of burgundy card stock
- 10½×11¼-inch pink card stock
- 11×8-inch piece of pink word-print paper
- card stock scraps in light and dark pink
- cream paper
- word stickers
- 3 round metal-edge tags
- assorted pink fibers and ribbons
- pink brads
- computer and printer
- scissors
- adhesive spacers, such as Pop Dots
- glue stick

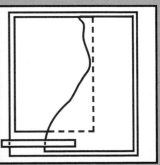

QUICK TIP

Cover the words of an old dog tag using alphabet stickers.

it's a teen thing

make it fast with an interesting headline and minimal embellishments on the rest of the page. Here alphabet bottle cap die cuts are used to spell the words. Raise a few of the die cuts with adhesive spacers.

materials

- photos
- 12-inch square of black card stock
- card stock in red and light green
- dog tags
- square tag
- ball chain
- alphabet bottle cap die cuts
- square silver brad
- green marker
- paper trimmer
- small paper punch
- decorative-edge scissors
- adhesive spacers, such as Pop Dots
- glue stick

Raise some of the letters with adhesive spacers.

Cut out a circle using decorative-edge scissors to resemble a bottle cap.

Use a square tag to frame a photo and hang from chain.

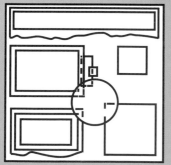

believe

make it fast by applying torn strips of scrapbook paper to accent one side of the photo, the tag, and the headline.

Detail the plaid strips with metal swirl paper clips.

materials

- photo
- 12-inch square of red card stock
- 12-inch square of red and green plaid scrapbook paper
- 12-inch square of black and white type scrapbook paper
- card stock scraps in red and cream
- fabric trim headline
- metal swirl paper clips
- brads
- fibers in red, green, and white
- paper punch
- computer and printer
- paper trimmer
- glue stick

Cut tag shapes, layer, punch a hole in the top, and thread with several fibers.

Fold over the end of the headline fabric and thread through a paper clip.

Tear one edge of scrapbook paper strip and fasten over the photo with brads.

madison

make it fast by pairing two coordinating big-print papers to frame a single photo. Divide the papers with a grosgrain ribbon and cut out two of the print images, such as the flowers, *below,* from the leftover paper.

materials

- photo
- two 12-inch squares of coordinating big-print papers
- yellow card stock
- 1-inch-wide yellow grosgrain ribbon
- 1×½-inch metal-edge white tag
- fine-line black marking pen
- paper trimmer
- scissors
- adhesive spacers, such as Pop Dots
- double-sided tape

Cover the paper seam with ribbon.

Use different print papers on the top and bottom of the page.

Use a marking pen to write a brief description on the tag. Attach with double-sided tape.

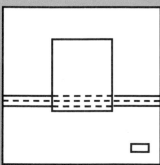

the great pumpkin

make it fast by cutting the mat larger on one side and folding that edge over the photo. To embellish, trim the flap with brads or stickers.

Use a photo marker to color in an important part of the photo, such as these pumpkins.

materials

- black-and-white photos
- 12-inch square of orange plaid paper
- thin cardboard
- orange small-print paper
- newsprint scrapbook paper
- twine
- brads
- number and alphabet stickers
- die-cut headline
- computer and printer
- ½-inch circle punch
- paper cutter
- photo markers in blue and orange
- glue stick

Fold over one edge of the cardboard mat.

Tear an opening in the newspaper mat and slip in the photo.

Wrap the photos with twine and knot on the front.

Punch out cardboard circles to back the alphabet stickers.

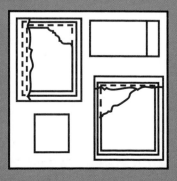

Use stickers to embellish the page corners.

patriotic play

make it fast by keeping trims to a minimum. The subtle patterns of the papers *below* create texture without overpowering the photos. To break up the background, use a contrasting paper, such as the red, on half of the page.

materials

- photos
- 12-inch square of blue polka-dot paper
- red check paper
- card stock in navy blue and white
- sticker border and corners
- small brads
- computer and printer
- small paper punch
- star punch
- paper cutter
- glue stick

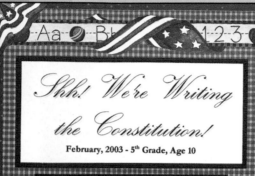

Shh! We're Writing the Constitution!

February, 2003 - 5th Grade, Age 10

Bailey says, "This show was fun because our class got to choreograph each of the songs, and we got to dress up like the colonists. There was an explosion of baby powder in the girds' bathroom because we were pouring the substance all over our heads to give us white hair!" The above picture of Madison Thompson and Bailey is a good illustration of this!

Bailey turned her Brownie vest inside out to create her costume for the part of the delegate from New Jersey. Her favorite line was "No-account Yankee!" She also sang a solo on "Critical Moment" and duets on "Shh! We're Writing the Constitution" and "The Best that We Could Do." This project was a fun blend of social studies and music.

 *Songs*

The Thing That Holds Us Together
We've Got to be One People
Critical Moment
Shh! We're Writing the Constitution
The Give & Take
The Best That We Could Do
The Thing That Holds Us Together (Reprise)

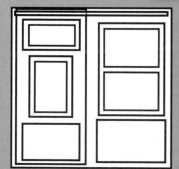

Use theme-related stickers to embellish the page corners.

Poke small brads through paper layers to secure them and highlight corner details.

Punch shapes from card stock to fill void areas on journal blocks.

nice guy

make it fast by wrinkling and tearing the papers. To create the look of leather, wrinkle card stock. To distress it further, tear a hole in it and turn back the edges around the hole. Tear a photo frame from red card stock, then roll back the edges of the opening.

QUICK TIP

To make the page shine, fold under the edges of a piece of metal mesh and use it to back journaling.

materials
■ photo
■ 12-inch square and scraps of red card stock
■ 12×5-inch piece of black card stock
■ metal mesh
■ eyelet-trim leather band
■ small silver brads
■ computer and printer
■ paper punch
■ scissors
■ double-sided tape

Scrunch and smooth black card stock to resemble leather.
■

Fold back the edges of a torn hole and place mesh behind opening.
■

Use brads to hold torn journaling box in place.
■

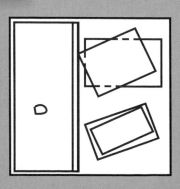

fudge mystery

make it fast by using squares of color. To make a checked background appearance, cut two squares from a color that contrasts with the background. Place them in opposite corners. Continue the square concept with small square paper accents and sharp square crops.

Apply a shadow option to a headline font for increased impact.

materials

- photos
- 12-inch squares of medium blue card stock
- card stock in royal blue, medium blue, white, and red
- blue chalk
- red eyelets and eyelet tool
- paper trimmer
- glue stick

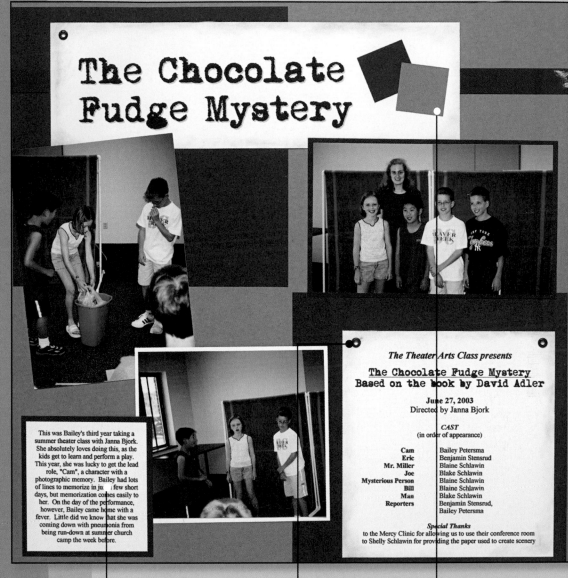

Use a computer to print journaling on a light color of card stock.

Attach program-like journaling with eyelets.

Overlap two small squares to give the headline intrigue.

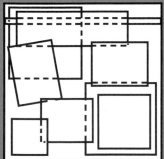

new friends

make it fast by combining two solid and two print papers. Balance the page by distributing the color and extending some shapes to the edge of the page. Print the headline and journaling on vellum to tell the story without completely concealing the background.

Use matching brads to attach the vellum headline.

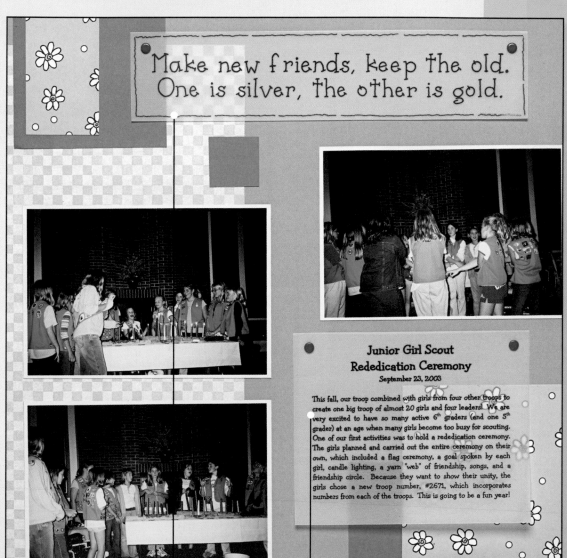

Make new friends, keep the old.
One is silver, the other is gold.

**Junior Girl Scout
Rededication Ceremony**
September 23, 2003

This fall, our troop combined with girls from four other troops to create one big troop of almost 20 girls and four leaders! We are very excited to have so many active 6th graders (and one 5th grader) at an age when many girls become too busy for scouting. One of our first activities was to hold a rededication ceremony. The girls planned and carried out the entire ceremony on their own, which included a flag ceremony, a goal spoken by each girl, candle lighting, a yarn "web" of friendship, songs, and a friendship circle. Because they want to show their unity, the girls chose a new troop number, #2671, which incorporates numbers from each of the troops. This is going to be a fun year!

materials
- photos
- 12-inch square of light teal card stock
- dark teal card stock
- 2 yellow print papers
- vellum
- small teal brads
- computer and printer
- paper trimmer
- small paper punch
- permanent fine-line black marking pen
- glue stick

Save yourself the hassle of mounting photos by leaving a white border when you crop them.

Use a permanent black marking pen to draw a quick border.

Print type on vellum to allow the background to show through.

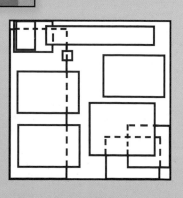

sep rams

make it fast by using strips of paper with a theme design to coordinate with the photos. Create a quick and easy scoreboard headline using one or two copies from art on page 169. Color in desired words with neon markers and fill in the rest with black.

materials

- photos
- two 12-inch squares of yellow card stock
- navy blue card stock
- color photocopy of basketball, letter, and scoreboard art, pages 167 and 169
- paper trimmer
- scissors
- non-bleeding bright neon markers
- black marker
- markers in team colors
- adhesive tabs

Art in back of book!

see page 169

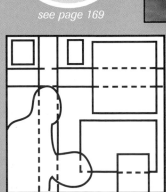

Silhouette enlargements for greater impact.

Use adhesive tabs to hold elements in place.

Overlap photos where there is a void in the photo.

QUICK TIP

Use a paper trimmer to cut strips quickly and accurately.

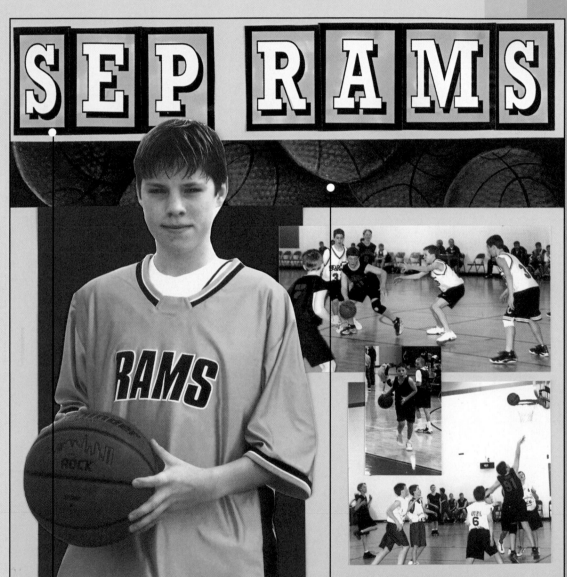

SEP RAMS

RAMS

Art in back of book!

E

see page 169

Enlarge the letters from page 167, cut out, and color with your team colors.

Enlarge the basketball border 115 percent to span a 12-inch page.

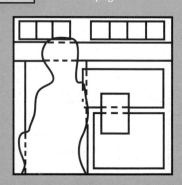

QUICK TIP

.mp

attended

Highlight the headline with a coordinating button tied with embroidery floss.

make it fast by using precut shapes and die cut embellishments. Place card stock triangles in the page corners to replicate the quiltlike die-cut designs.

materials

- photos
- 12-inch square of white card stock
- card stock in dark blue, dark red, and white
- precut dark red triangles
- quilt-theme die cuts
- red heart button
- blue embroidery floss
- sewing needle
- computer and printer
- paper trimmer
- glue stick

American Girl Camp
July 8-12, 2002 • Age 9

This summer, Bailey and Maddie Mandsager attended American Girl Camp at Gloria Dei Lutheran Church in Des Moines. This turned out to be a total craft immersion, as the girls made numerous projects each day related to one of the *American Girl* stories. Among many other things, they painted china (for Samantha's story), sewed a sampler (Kirsten), made a Mexican tin box (Josefina), decorated a frame with stamps around the world (Kit), and beaded American flag pins to represent girls of today.

a patchwork of friends

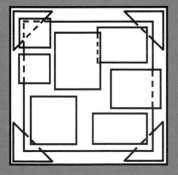

Place card stock triangles in the page corners.

Double-mat your favorite photo.

When necessary mount die cuts on card stock so they stand out from the background.

Print the headline and journaling in one block for efficiency.

drummer girl

make it fast by picking gray color-block background paper to organize the layout. Use the sections to arrange the components, overlapping the sections if desired, such as done with the journal box on the lower left of the page.

DrUMMer GirL

materials

- photos
- 12-inch square of gray color-block card stock
- card stock in black, gray, and white
- computer and printer
- paper cutter
- glue stick

Bailey, you have been given an incredible gift of musical talent. Music comes so naturally to you, and I am amazed by how quickly you have progressed. We are so delighted that you have taken up percussion in addition to your piano. What a special thing for you and your dad to be able to share this interest. With his expertise guiding you, you'll never "play like a girl!" Just remember to cherish and develop your special gift and it will be with you for a lifetime.

March, 2003 | Age 10 | 5th Grade

"If a man does not keep pace with his companions, perhaps it is because he hears a different drummer. Let him keep step to the music he hears, however measured and far away."
- *Thoreau*

Double-mat one photo to be the central focus of the page.

Align two photos of the same size.

Use a quote that relates to the theme.

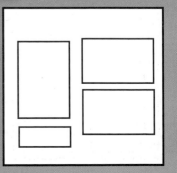

Turn square eyelets on point to make them appear as diamonds.

make it fast using paper strips—just one sheet of card stock yields several. These make great page borders and are spectacular when accented with tiny paper rectangles and square eyelets.

materials

- photos
- 12-inch square of dark brown card stock
- card stock in white, red, and yellow
- square black eyelets
- eyelet tool
- branch rubber stamp
- dark red ink
- computer and printer
- paper trimmer
- glue stick

AFRICAN TALES

Theatre Arts Class – June, 2001
The Leopard's Noisy Drum
Who's in Rabbit's House?

Bailey participated in Janna Bjork's Theatre Arts class this summer. Her group memorized two African folktale plays, and created masks, African art and props in just a week. Bailey played the role of the Lion and Rhinoceros. They performed both plays for parents on Friday. As you can see from the pictures here, she loved the experience and plans to do it again next summer. Her friends Brynn Schor and Lexie Swift (third and fifth from left) were part of this class. Bailey has gained a lot of respect for her teacher Janna, a local high school student who plans to enter the teaching profession.

Silhouette an image from your photos.

Accent the journal box with a stamped image.

Print journaling so it wraps around a photo.

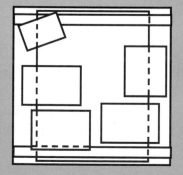

two home runs

make it fast using easy personalization techniques. Use the baseball art provided on page 169. Write a name on the ball using a marking pen. To make the headline, cut out the appropriate letters and adhere them in a row at the bottom of the page.

materials
- photo
- 12-inch square of green scrapbook paper
- paper to back silhouette, if needed
- blue card stock
- color photocopy of baseball art, page 169
- marking pens in black and 2 colors to coordinate with photo
- scissors
- paper trimmer
- glue stick

Art in back of book!

see page 169

Use marking pen to personalize the baseball.

Run the stripe to the edge of the page.

Glue letters side by side to form headline.

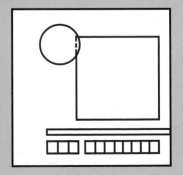

Draw a speech bubble on card stock and trim for a personal remark.

can I have a cow?

make it fast by tearing pieces of mulberry paper to create an animal skin look for the background. Brown mulberry paper is used here to resemble a cow's coat, but choose any color and tear it into spot shapes or stripes to depict the appropriate animal fur.

materials

- photos
- two 12-inch squares of white card stock
- brown mulberry paper
- 8½×11-inch paper to coordinate with photos
- blue card stock
- fine- and medium-tip black marking pens
- scissors
- paper trimmer
- glue stick

Place some of the photos to extend beyond the 8½×11-inch paper.

Choose a contrasting paper to separate the photos from the background.

Cut a speech bubble from white card stock and write a comment with marking pen.

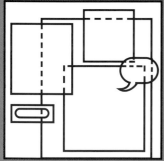

my baby

make it fast by writing a headline with an opaque marking pen and printing an in-depth journal box. These components, combined with a large and a small photo, are all you need for a successful page.

Dress up photo corners by trimming with a pair of decorative-edge corner scissors.

my baby

ne spring the raccoons kept t king the goose eggs from the nests on Mike's pond and then the mother disappeared. We took the eggs from the nest and put them in an incubator and in about 3 weeks we had 2 baby goslings who just loved Emma and Emma loved them. They ate our flowers and grew and grew. Emma kissed them goodbye as we took them to Uncle John's pond to turn them loose. They ate all his flowers too. Impatiens were their favorites. They flew in to town one day, walked through the neighborhood (We assume they cleaned out some flower beds there also.) and walked up to the people inside the gas station. Fall came and they flew away south. When we see a flock of geese on the pond now, we always wonder if we know them.

materials
- photos
- 12-inch square of scrapbook paper
- coordinating solid card stock
- subtle-print scrapbook paper for journal box
- opaque marking pen
- circle cutter
- scissors
- paper trimmer
- decorative-edge corner scissors
- computer and printer
- glue stick

Print journaling to wrap around a circular photo.

Choose a color of opaque marker that shows up on the background.

Crop the small photo into a circle, silhouetting a detail to extend onto the mat.

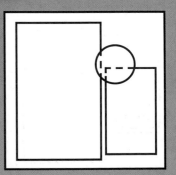

Use a stencil and a white opaque marking pen to outline letters for a short headline.

ben

make it fast by using three similar photos in graduated sizes. Place the photos on the page to overlap in a diagonal configuration. Counterbalance the photos by placing die cuts that match the theme in the open corners.

materials

- 3 photos in graduated sizes
- 12-inch square of dark blue card stock
- gold subtle-print paper
- leaf die cuts or color photocopies of leaves
- alphabet stencil
- scissors
- paper trimmer
- white opaque marking pen
- glue stick

Run the die cuts off the page and trim even with page edge. ■

Use a plate to draw guidelines for curved lettering. ■

Trim letters to allow a white outline to show. ■

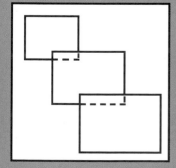

visit with santa

make it fast by using premade art accents on page 171. Photocopy and combine the swirl paper, tags, border, and corner triangles to make a magical holiday page.

QUICK TIP

Use a punch to create stars from photocopies of holiday art.

Our Visit with Santa

Christmas 2001

Ryan asked the jolly ol' fellow for a magic set and a football. On Morgan's list was a dolly, books, and a kitty (stuffed or real!).

materials

- photo
- 12-Inch square of red card stock
- color photocopies of the holiday art, page 171
- pale yellow parchment
- star punch
- scissors
- computer and printer
- glue stick

Art in back of book!

see page 171

Accent the page with stars punched from the photocopies and parchment.

Center a corner mount at the bottom of the journal box.

Align the journal box with the date.

Silhouette a figure from a tag to finish off the border strip.

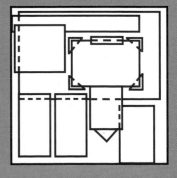

QUICK TIP

Thread textured yarn through a charm for a stunning accent.

make it fast by adding beads. Choose a premade dimensional baby bracelet (or make your own) and edge the journal box with strips of micro beads.

materials

- photo
- 12-inch square of blue card stock
- 12-inch square of baby-print scrapbook paper
- light green card stock
- blue and pink textured yarn
- safety pin charm
- baby bracelet dimensional trim
- micro beads
- ¼-inch-wide double-sided tape
- computer and printer
- paper trimmer
- glue stick
- thick white crafts glue

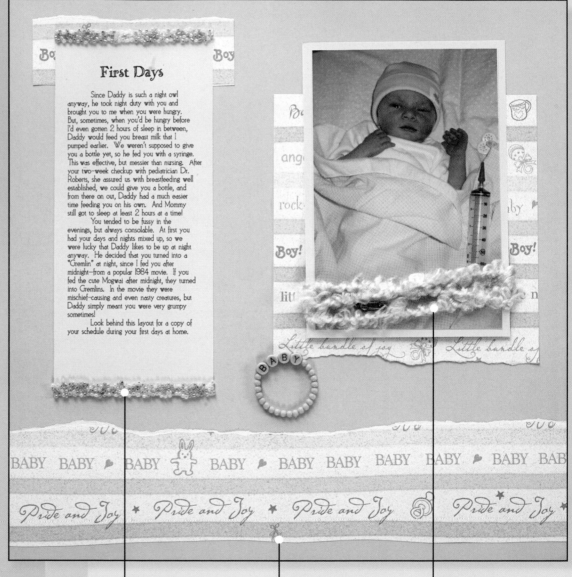

First Days

Since Daddy is such a night owl anyway, he took night duty with you and brought you to me when you were hungry. But, sometimes, when you'd be hungry before I'd even gotten 2 hours of sleep in between, Daddy would feed you breast milk that I pumped earlier. We weren't supposed to give you a bottle yet, so he fed you with a syringe. This was effective, but messier than nursing. After your two-week checkup with pediatrician Dr. Roberts, she assured us with breastfeeding well established, we could give you a bottle, and from there on out, Daddy had a much easier time feeding you on his own. And Mommy still got to sleep at least 2 hours at a time!

You tended to be fussy in the evenings, but always consolable. At first you had your days and nights mixed up, so we were lucky that Daddy likes to be up at night anyway. He decided that you turned into a "Gremlin" at night, since I fed you after midnight—from a popular 1984 movie. If you fed the cute Mogwai after midnight, they turned into Gremlins. In the movie they were mischief-causing and even nasty creatures, but Daddy simply meant you were very grumpy sometimes!

Look behind this layout for a copy of your schedule during your first days at home.

Place strips of double-sided tape at the top and bottom of the journal box and cover them with micro beads.

Trim one long edge irregularly and tear the other.

Wrap the photo with yarn threaded through a charm.

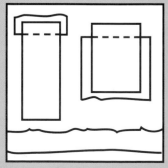

blocks

make it fast by using coordinating buttons for accents. For detail, tie them with embroidery floss or mount them on small card stock squares.

Derek received these blocks for his first birthday. The kids can play with them for hours! The box, of course, is also a big hit. Brynn and Derek are such great buddies right now!

be
glad
of life.

- Henry van Dyke

BLOCKS

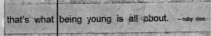

that's what being young is all about.   – ruby dee

buddies

materials

- photos
- 12-inch square blue polka-dot paper
- coordinating stripe paper
- white card stock
- alphabet template
- blue buttons
- embroidery floss
- sewing needle
- stickers in rickrack and phrase motifs
- vellum
- eyelets
- eyelet tool
- computer and printer
- paper trimmer
- scissors
- glue stick
- thick white crafts glue

Use a word sticker below the box.
■

Use a template to make letters for the headline.
■

Print journaling in a color to coordinate with page.
■

Accent copy blocks with eyelets.
■

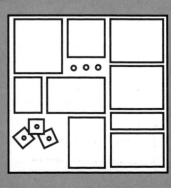

Place stickers where papers overlap to help hold papers in place.

best friends

make it fast by printing the headline on light color background paper. To embellish the page, place stickers and paper triangles in an artistic arrangement around the photo.

materials

- photo
- 12-inch square of pink card stock
- 11½-inch square of lavender textured card stock
- 8½×11-inch piece of pink parchment paper
- metallic gold paper
- heart vellum stickers
- scissors
- computer and printer
- glue stick

me & my

Best Friends

Balance the photo with careful sticker placement.

Layer papers to make a quick background.

Crop the photo to leave a white border, if possible.

Use scissors to cut triangles from metallic gold paper.

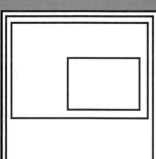

girly girl

make it fast by combining premade items. Incorporate adhesive mesh, brads, button motifs strung on yarn, and a slide mount—all to coordinate with your papers. Punch out a headline and handwrite the journaling to make it super quick.

QUICK TIP

Punch holes in die cuts and thread with yarn, string, narrow ribbon, or embroidery floss.

GIRLY GIRL

Megan, you have grown into such a beautiful young lady. I couldn't get over the blueness of your eyes. So pretty! Your daddy is going to have his handsfull as you get older, keeping boys in line. Being the first of only 2 girls in the Franklin family will all help advise dad.

Use a slide mount for personalization. ■

Accent mesh strips using brads. ■

Use patterns on page 152 to make buttons from card stock. ■

Arrange punched letters in a random, tipped fashion. ■

materials

- photo; 12-inch square of black card stock
- 12-inch square of button-print paper
- card stock in bright colors; yellow yarn
- adhesive yellow mesh, such as Magic Mesh
- color brads
- pink slide mount
- alphabet punches
- paper punch
- tracing paper; pencil
- paper trimmer
- black marking pen
- scissors; glue stick
- adhesive spacers

Patterns in back of book

see page 152

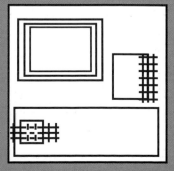

Cute as a Bug!

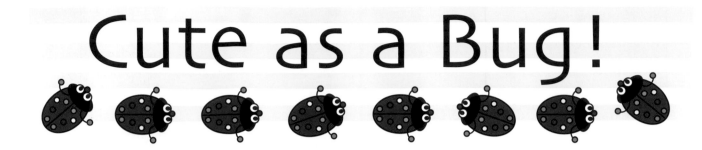

sweet baby girl

sweet baby boy

OH, BABY!

rock-a-bye baby

Sweet thing!

Kids Do the Cutest Things!

girly girl

ALL BOY

Are you cute or what?

Children Are a Blessing

Having Fun with the kids

Capture those giggling, fun, frolicking, adventurous, memory-making, heartwarming family times on scrapbook pages that tug at your heartstrings.

family fun &
play with pets

☐ pla

Offset journal strips on darker card stock rectangles to create the look of a shadow.

polly and emma

make it fast using one large photo and labels printed from a computer. A lighthearted photo works well with this layout and is enhanced by the humorous option statements at the top of the page.

materials
- large photo
- 12-inch square of gold subtle-print scrapbook paper
- purple scrapbook paper
- white paper
- mulberry papers in black and metallic brown
- purple marking pen
- computer and printer
- paper trimmer
- glue stick

☐ planting trees   ☐ burying bones

☐ looking for treasures

☒ just diggin

Polly and Emma

Type a check-off box before each statement.

Tear and layer mulberry paper to resemble dirt.

Mount the photo and journaling on contrasting papers.

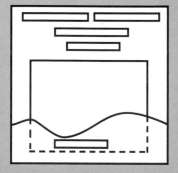

emma & honey

make it fast with photo frames. These coordinating frames are provided on pages 161 and 177. Cut them out and layer them on additional papers to make the page rich with color.

QUICK TIP

Use a loop of gold jumpring to hang a paper tag from ½-inch-wide ribbon.

materials

- photos; 12-inch square of green polka-dot paper
- rust subtle-pattern scrapbook paper
- dark green card stock
- color photocopy of mats and tag, pages 161 and 177
- ½-inch-wide gold and burgundy ribbon
- gold jumpring
- paper punch
- paper trimmer
- black marking pen
- crafts knife; glue stick

Art in back of book!

see pages 161 and 177

Punch a hole in the top edge of the tag. Thread ribbon through a jumpring; attach the tag.

Fold ribbon back and forth vertically on the page, adhering in spots with glue stick.

Trim a wider green mat to the back provided decorative mat. Cut out the frame center using a crafts knife.

tinsel

make it fast by using a catchy subhead to direct the page. Look at advertisements and watch commercials for inspiration; then continue the thought in the journaling.

materials

- photos
- 12-inch square of white card stock
- 12×6¼-inch rectangle of teal card stock
- card stock in black and white
- teal brads
- small paper punch
- paper trimmer
- computer and printer
- glue stick

T I N S E L:
She's Everywhere You Want to Be

......on the chair, in the towels, on the wrapping paper, on the dining room table, in the drawer, in the cupboard, under the couch, under the bed, on the kitchen table, in the pantry, in the tent, in the bathtub, on the dryer, in the sink, on the scrapbook table, in the dollhouse, under the ottoman, in the linen closet, on the dining room chair, in the rocking chair, in the shower, in the sock drawer, in the scrapbooking tote, on the closet shelf, on the stove, on the mantel, on top of the recliner, on the bed, on the back of the couch, on the back of the chair, on the bench, in the baby crib, in the doll crib, in the computer desk.......

Crop three photos the same height and align side by side.

Cut two strips and join end to end to run the width of the page.

Leave room below the title for a block of journaling.

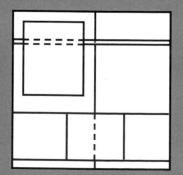

our dog t-bone

make it fast by using premade borders and accents. The versatile strips at the top and bottom of this page are available on page 152. The die cuts and dimensional stickers are sprinkled across the layout to increase interest.

Layer precut color card stock squares and place behind a photo to draw attention to it.

A Puppy At Last! We got our puppy on November 1, 2003 from a breeder near Iowa City. The kids decided to name the little cutie 'T-Bone. He is so gentle and must be the most lovable dog in the whole world!

best friend

doggie bones

dog training made easy!

materials

- photo
- 12-inch square of yellow card stock
- 12×5-inch rectangle of grass-print paper
- 2½-inch square of red card stock
- 3-inch square of orange card stock
- 4½-inch square of yellow card stock
- 3×4-inch piece of red card stock
- vellum; color marking pens
- photocopies of border pattern, page 152
- dog-theme die cuts and dimensional stickers; scissors
- computer and printer
- spray adhesive
- glue stick

Print the headline and journaling on vellum; crop to desired size.

Incorporate a sticker into the headline.

Use marking pens to color in the photocopied border from page 152.

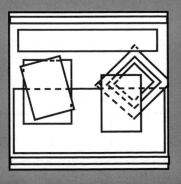

Cut a triangle from contrasting paper, overlap, and write the headline across the papers.

day in the field

make it fast by assembling premade mats and borders. These outdoorsy prints are on page 173 to photocopy and use again and again.

materials

- photos
- 12-inch square of paper to coordinate with art, page 173
- 8½×11-inch piece of paper to contrast background paper
- green scrapbook paper
- color photocopy of desired art, page 173
- crafts knife; computer and printer
- tracing paper; pencil
- green colored pencil
- glue stick

Art in back of book!

see page 173

Use a crafts knife to cut out the center of the mat.

Cut a photo into a diamond shape and mount on a colored piece of paper.

Computer-generate the headline and trace the outline onto the background papers.

Shade in the headline using a colored pencil.

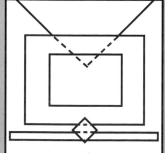

great-grandmother

make it fast by applying vellum stickers to accent the headline and the journal box. Vellum offers subtle color and design while allowing the background to show through.

Summer '88

Christmas '87

Great-Grandma Johnson loved seeing the great-grandkids. Anytime we came home, someone would go to Clinton and get Grandma.

LOVE

Great-Grandmothers
Are Angels in Disguise

materials
- photos
- 12-inch square of green card stock
- yellow card stock
- vellum
- vellum stickers
- chalk in black and dark yellow
- computer and printer
- paper trimmer
- glue stick

Print type on vellum and chalk the edges for character.

Overlap one or two stickers on each journal box.

Place the photos at the top and balance with the headline at the bottom.

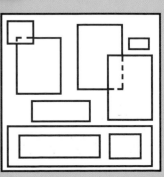

"Ground" animal stickers and die cuts by placing them on torn paper "grass."

ride 'em cowboy

make it fast by mounting the photos aligned on one card stock rectangle. This presentation groups the photos as a unit to create a clean layout.

materials

- photos
- 12-inch square of leatherlike navy blue card stock
- card stock in tan and two shades of green
- 12-inch strip of ½-inch-wide stitched suede trim
- horse die cut
- computer and printer
- corner rounder
- paper trimmer
- thick white crafts glue
- glue stick

Wendy called to invite us along on the People Place adventure at Blacks Heritage Farm. We saw dogs, kittens, goats, turkeys, chickens, llamas, Chinese chickens with hair, not feathers and an extra toe on each foot (!), a white deer, and more! The largest goat's name was Scooby-he was cute, but VERY pushy when it came to attention and food.

You had the cute, interested but befuddled look on your face much of the time-what ARE those things, Mom? You even sat on the pony and held the saddle. After the pony, we all settled in for a hayrack ride around the farm and gardens. You fell asleep about ten seconds after I sat down-it's hard work riding a pony.

Ride 'em, Cowboy!

Use crafts glue to hold suede trim in place.

Combine fonts for an interesting headline.

Use a corner rounder on the headline paper.

Tear a piece of green paper to look like grass.

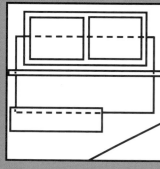

grampa's lake

make it fast by butting photos together to create a square. Separate the photos by adhering decorative strips over the seams. All the art embellishments for this page, including the plaid strips, are provided on page 175.

QUICK TIP

Use scissors to cut out the plaid strips within the heavy black outlines.

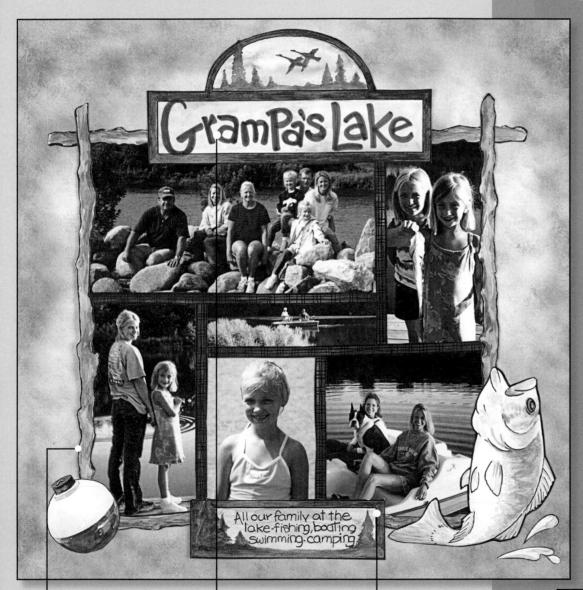

materials
- photos
- 12-inch square of green watercolor-style scrapbook paper
- color photocopy of desired art on page 175
- scissors
- paper trimmer
- wide-tip green marking pen
- fine-line black marking pen
- glue stick

Art in back of book!

see page 175

Use the stick art from page 175 to form a border around photos.

Write your headline and journaling with markers.

Center the journal box at the bottom of the page.

File stickers alphabetically by subject to find motifs quickly.

first snow

make it fast by using stickers and an easy-to-make vertical border. The pattern to make snowman faces is on page 152. Speed up the process by asking the kids to create the frosty fellows for you.

materials

- photos
- 12-inch square of blue card stock
- card stock in white and blue
- photocopy of snowman patterns, page 152
- snowflake stickers
- computer and printer
- colored pencils
- circle cutter
- paper trimmer
- glue stick

Patterns in back of book!

see page 152

The first snow of the season and the boys couldn't wait to go outside and play, even the "biggest boy". They had a great time sledding and throwing snow. When this Iowa snow was to cold to play in any longer hot chocolate was the warmth for these little snowmen.

Use the pattern on page 152 to make snowmen faces; color with pencils.

Use a computer to print journaling on white card stock.

Place snowflake stickers to embellish open areas.

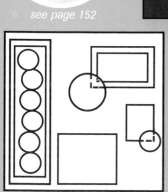

rough & tough

make it fast by printing the headline and journaling on acetate. This allows you to use different fonts and sizes of type and lets the background show through.

Rough & Tough

Rock Throwing....

Dirt Kicking....

FROG CATCHING....

Dad Wrestling....

Dog Chasing....

Car Loving....

Cute as a Bug.......

BOY!

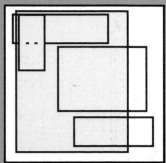

materials

- photo
- 12-inch square of light blue card stock
- 8½×11-inch sheet of acetate
- lightweight cardboard
- white paper tag and light blue envelope
- metal mesh
- washers
- brads
- alphabet stickers
- blue button
- swirl paper clip
- fibers in blue and brown
- scissors
- small paper punch
- computer and printer
- paper trimmer
- glue stick

Use a brad to attach each washer. Embellish the brad with an alphabet sticker.

Plan the headline to fall to the right of center and the journaling to wrap the photo.

Cut mesh rectangles and fold under the frayed edges.

93

Note: gray area indicates top acetate sheet.

Outline your own art elements with a wide black marking pen to make cropping easy.

my cat

make it fast with a large colorful photo frame and a single photo. The pretty frame, headline, and journal heart are provided on pages 177 and 179. Photocopy the art elements to use them several times.

materials

- photo
- 12-inch square of blue polka-dot paper
- color photocopy of art, page 177 and 179
- scissors
- black marking pen
- tape
- glue stick

Art in back of book!

see pages 177 and 179

Use scissors to cut a slightly wavy line around art elements from pages 177 and 179.

Use a marking pen for personalization.

Glue the photo and frame slightly below the page center.

cat sitter

make it fast by combining embellishments with solid color papers. The print elements, *below,* are available on page 181. Team these charming accents with blues and tans for a beautifully quick page.

QUICK TIP

...ken on one c...
...e very well cared for!

Use a paper punch to make a starter hole for eyelets.

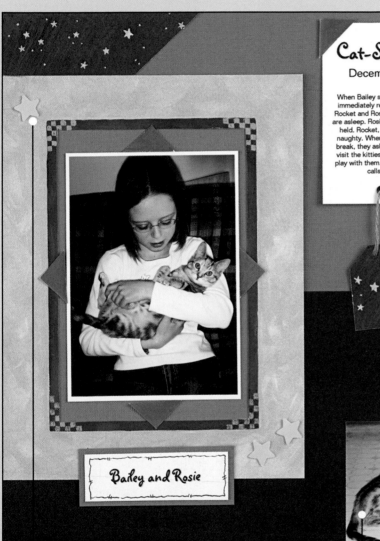

Cat-Sitter Extraordinaire

December, 2003 | Bailey, age 10

When Bailey started babysitting for the Hausers this fall, she immediately recognized one of the benefits: their two kitties, Rocket and Rosie. Bailey loves playing with them after the kids are asleep. Rosie, the calico female, is so cuddly and loves to be held. Rocket, the black male, is very friendly but sometimes naughty. When the Hausers went on vacation over Christmas break, they asked Bailey to cat-sit. She was only too happy to visit the kitties each day to feed them, change their litter, and play with them. These pictures were taken on one of her house calls. The kitties were very well cared for!

Bailey and Rosie

materials

- photos; 12-inch squares of 3 coordinating scrapbook papers, plus white and yellow
- color photocopy of art elements, page 181
- round and star paper punches; eyelets and eyelet tool; scissors
- light blue fibers
- computer and printer
- black fine-line marking pen
- paper trimmer
- glue stick

Art in back of book!

see page 181

Use a star punch to make accents from yellow paper.

Place the darkest color of card stock on the bottom of the page for weight.

Leave a photo unmounted if it contrasts with the paper color.

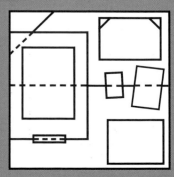

christmas with sam

make it fast using the art from page 183. These winter and check designs work well with any playful scrapbook page theme. Use one of the art boxes for the headline.

materials

- photos
- two 12-inch squares of dark red card stock
- red check print paper
- card stock in black, cream, and dark red
- color photocopy of art, page 183
- paper trimmer
- paper punch; scissors
- computer and printer
- square punch; cream fibers; temporary adhesive
- adhesive spacers, such a Pop Dots
- glue stick

Christmas with Sam
- December, 2002 -

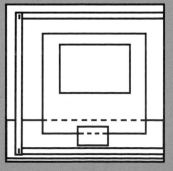

Mount a mitten silhouette on black paper and trim a narrow border.

Print comments on designed journal box by attaching box to paper with temporary adhesive before printing.

Layer punched squares on larger check-print squares.

Aunt Carole's cat, Sam, is so huge! We measured his middle and found that he is 26 inches around - bigger than Bailey's waist! We had fun seeing him at Christmas, especially when we found him out on the porch in Aunt Carole's Christmas village. As large as he is, he looked even bigger next to those tiny houses!

Crop two photos the same size and align.

Loop fibers through hole in tag.

Art in back of book!

see page 183

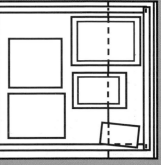

Ask your photo developer to print photos with a white edge to save time matting.

croppy cat

make it fast with stickers. Arrange alphabet stickers in a wavy fashion to make headline placement easy. For added charm, use theme stickers across the top of the page and at corners of the journal box.

materials

- photos
- 12-inch squares of card stock in green and white
- card stock scraps in dark red, green, and gold
- check scrapbook paper
- small silver brads
- alphabet stickers
- scrapbook-theme stickers
- small paper punch
- computer and printer
- paper trimmer
- glue stick

Anchor a check strip with stickers..

Use a larger and bolder font for the journaling subhead.

Cut journal box large enough to overlap a corner with stickers.

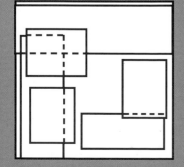

all I need to know

make it fast using several photos on a two-color background. Crop the journaling into small rectangles for playful positioning.

Offset a 10-inch square of contrasting paper to jazz up the background.

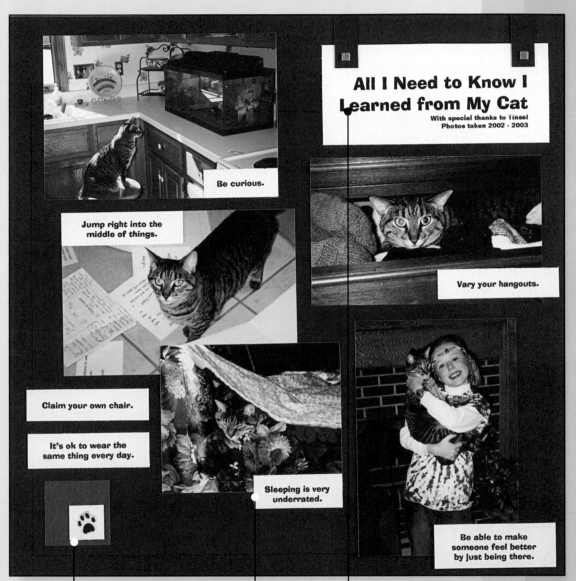

All I Need to Know I Learned from My Cat

With special thanks to Tinsel
Photos taken 2002 - 2003

Be curious.

Jump right into the middle of things.

Vary your hangouts.

Claim your own chair.

It's ok to wear the same thing every day.

Sleeping is very underrated.

Be able to make someone feel better by just being there.

materials

- photos
- 12-inch square of navy card stock
- 10-inch square of dark red card stock
- scraps of card stock in white, blue, and dark red
- square brads
- paw print sticker
- computer and printer
- small paper punch
- paper trimmer
- glue stick

Mount a sticker on layered card stock.

Overlap photos with labels.

Make your headline look like a sign by placing two small rectangles and brads at the top of the headline block.

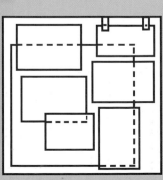

FAMILY FUN

Having a ball!

Our Goofy Gang

Our Kitty

Our Puppy

Is this fun or what?!

I won't tell if you won't...I won't tell if you won't...I won't tell if you won't...I won't tell if you won't...I won't tell if you won't...I won't tell if you won't...

 **FAMILY IS THE FABRIC OF LIFE**

Sisterly Love

brotherly love

 **Good Ol' Mom**

Good Ol' Dad

■ ■ ■ ■ ■

Ski, swim, travel, sightsee, hike, play, explore, shop, walk, visit, golf— whatever you like to do for fun, these creative on-the-go pages are inspired by recreation.

places to go,
things to do

fun at the lake

make it fast using several photos without mats. Leave space near the center of the photo grouping to create a scene made with stickers.

Print a headline on vellum to allow the background to show through.

materials

- photos
- 12-inch square of white card stock
- vellum
- photocopy of sun pattern, page 153
- beach-theme stickers
- colored pencils
- computer and printer
- scissors
- paper trimmer
- glue stick

Art in back of book!

see page 153

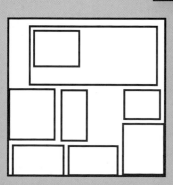

Use stickers to reinforce the theme. Attach vellum to the background using stickers.

Crop photos to fill the lower half of the page, allowing narrow borders.

Use the sun pattern to draw a sun on a strip of card stock. Color in the sun and rays with colored pencils. Cut and color a strip for "water" if desired. Print the headline on vellum and adhere to in the open area.

riding the waves

make it fast without using any embellishments. Mount some of the photos on colorful card stock. Then arrange them and a pair of paper strips around the headline.

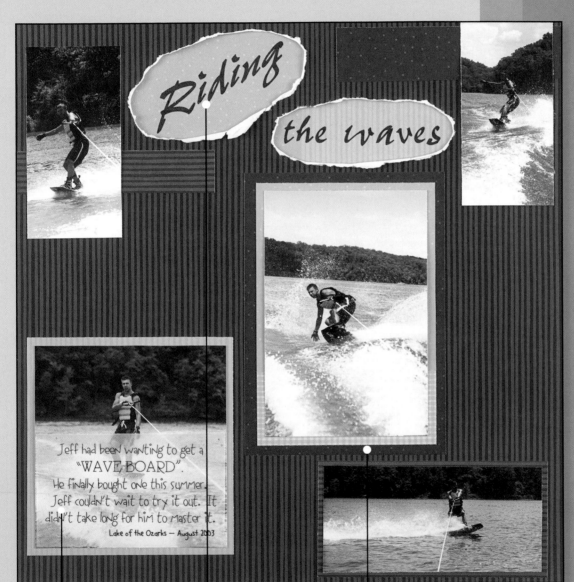

Riding the waves

Jeff had been wanting to get a "WAVE BOARD".
He finally bought one this summer. Jeff couldn't wait to try it out. It didn't take long for him to master it.
Lake of the Ozarks — August 2003

materials
- photos
- 12-inch square of blue striped card stock
- subtle-pattern card stock in red and yellow
- vellum
- paper trimmer
- computer and printer
- tape
- glue stick

Print journaling on vellum and place on top of a photo.

Print the headline words on yellow card stock and trim leaving wide borders. Tear holes in the blue background paper and tape the headline underneath.

Double-mount the main photo.

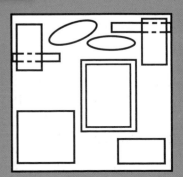

black hills railroad

make it fast using color-block printed paper. This type of paper has such details as the headline area, photo mats, and tags printed on the paper. Rotate the background paper to suit your page.

Make the pre-printed blocks look more dimensional using fiber and eyelets.

materials

- Photos
- 12-inch square of color-block paper
- card stock in white and black
- black brads
- silver eyelets and eyelet tool
- white, gray, and black fiber
- paper punch
- computer and printer
- paper trimmer
- glue stick
- tape

RIDE THE BLACK HILLS
-- CENTRAL RAILROAD --
June, 2002

On this chilly, drizzly Saturday morning, we took a leisurely ride on the Black Hills Central Railroad. The train took a winding path through the beautiful Black Hills. Out of the windows, we could see lush forests and rocky streams.

104

Use the measuring guides on the back of the background paper to create the headline and journaling strip.

Cut a scenic photo into thirds and place on tags. Punch holes in the top of each tag and secure eyelets in the holes.

Thread fiber through to eyelets; tape the ends on the page back.

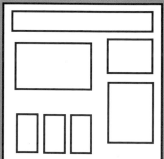

sod house

make it fast by printing a computer-generated title and journaling to start off this historic page. To create an aged look, darken the edges of the papers with brown chalk. Tear and chalk the edges of the photo mats to contribute character and a vintage look to the page.

Combine fibers and raffia to create a natural look.

materials
- photos
- 12-inch squares of sage green and dark sage green card stock
- tan card stock scraps
- nature-theme paper cutout
- raffia
- brown chenille string
- eyelets; eyelet tool
- brown chalk
- computer and printer
- iron
- paper trimmer
- glue stick
- tape

SOD HOUSE
~~~ On the Prairie ~~~

June 11, 2002

Near Walnut Grove, Minnesota are two prairie soddies that have been constructed on a private farm. These sod houses are similar to Laura's dugout on Plum Creek, except hers was built into a hill. Made of sod "bricks", the walls are two feet thick, and grass grows on some of the roofs. Inside the houses during the day, it is extremely cool and very dark. The only way to light these soddies is to use oil lamps. We visited the soddies to get a feel for what some types of prairie houses were like. Grandma decided that she'd like to go back sometime and spend the night in one, but Bailey preferred more modern accommodations! After this stop, we would soon be on our way home from our wonderful ~~~~~ vacation. We are very grateful to Grandma and ~~~ ~~~ on this adventure!

· THE PRAIRIE DUGOUT ·

Wet, crinkle, and iron card stock to make a textured background paper.

Combine two types of fibers—paper raffia and soft chenille string. Tape raffia ends to the back of the page.

Tear paper edges and rub them with brown chalk.

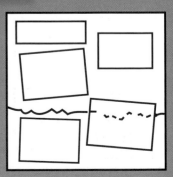

Use different sizes of the same font to print the headline and journaling boxes.

materials

- photos
- 12-inch square of theme-print paper
- card stock in yellow and white
- water-theme sticker
- blue fine-line marking pen
- circle cutter
- oval cutter
- scissors
- glue stick

skiing

make it fast using circle and oval cutters. Crop several photos with these tools, place the photos on a theme background paper, and you're almost done.

Group photos of the same person to share one label.

Arrange photos on page to leave room for the headline and labels.

Mount a sticker on card stock and edge with a broken line using a marking pen.

tidelands

make it fast by color-blocking to organize pages quickly and easily. Skip the photo mats and arrange photos and card stock pieces in a geometric design for a stylized scrapbook page.

Highlight special items from photos by silhouetting them and placing them in corners.

tidelands

NATURE CENTER

Wednesday, June 11, 2003

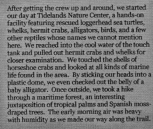

After getting the crew up and around, we started our day at Tidelands Nature Center, a hands-on facility featuring rescued loggerhead sea turtles, whelks, hermit crabs, alligators, birds, and a few other reptiles whose names we cannot mention here. We reached into the cool water of the touch tank and pulled out hermit crabs and whelks for closer examination. We touched the shells of horseshoe crabs and looked at all kinds of marine life found in the area. By sticking our heads into a plastic dome, we even checked out the belly of a baby alligator. Once outside, we took a hike through a maritime forest, an interesting juxtaposition of tropical palms and Spanish moss-draped trees. The early morning air was heavy with humidity as we made our way along the trail.

materials

- photos
- 12-inch square of brown card stock
- tan card stock
- scrap of brown card stock
- eyelets and eyelet tool
- shell stickers
- paper trimmer
- computer and printer
- brown chalk
- scissors
- glue stick
- adhesive spacers, such as Pop Dots

Group theme-related stickers on a card stock rectangle, raising one or two of the stickers from the background using adhesive spacers.

Accent card stock pieces with eyelets.

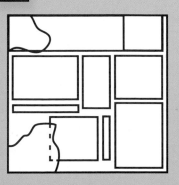

the badlands

make it fast by overlapping blocks of solid card stock to make a background for scenic photos. For the quickest method, use a paper trimmer or purchased precut pieces of card stock. Choose two or three colors to unify the pages and to minimize cost.

materials

- photos
- two 12-inch squares of cream card stock
- card stock in rust, olive, and tan
- cream vellum
- alphabet die cut machine
- eyelets and eyelet tool
- computer and printer
- paper trimmer
- glue stick

Create a bold headline from coordinating card stock using a die cut machine.

Use eyelets to produce artistic details on the card stock.

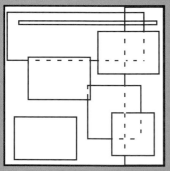

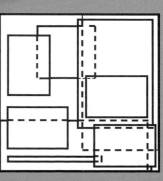
QUICK TIP

Thursday, June 6, 2002
You are driving throug
in the far distance, yo
so distinct from t
Grandpa, Bailey

Print type on vellum to allow the background to show through subtly.

Thursday, June 6, 2002
You are driving through the rather non-descript South Dakota plains when suddenly, in the far distance, you see the Badlands rising up on the horizon. The landforms are so distinct from the surrounding area that it takes you by surprise. Grandma, Grandpa, Bailey and I stopped and hiked along a trail with stunning views of the Badlands. I was awestruck by the layers of colors visible in the deep gorges and jagged ridges. Later that evening, we went back to the visitors' center to watch an outdoor slideshow about the history of buffalo hunting in the area. We learned a great deal about the plight of the buffalo and their place in the lives of Native Americans. The amphitheater was an incredible setting for this show. As the sun set, the colors around us deepened and glowed. We camped that night at the Badlands White River KOA Kampground. It was a lovely area, and we could walk down to the shallow river bed. We all had a good laugh when we came back to the camper and found it was full of moths!

Overlap card stock squares and rectangles to create a layered look. These card stock shapes are often available as precut pieces.

the best day

make it fast using large photographs that display drama. Crop one photo horizontally the width of the page. Silhouette another photo that has an interesting shape.

materials
- photos
- 12-inch square of orange card stock
- 12-inch square of bright blue card stock
- card stock scraps in orange, green, red, and yellow
- permanent black marking pen
- scissors
- paper trimmer
- glue stick

"I loved Legoland. It was the best. There were lots of buttons to push. Everything was made of legos. Miniland was my favorite. It had skyscrapers the Statue of Liberty, trains that really moved, legos that squirted water. I got to sit in a jungle jeep, get inside a lions mouth, and write my name in legos. It was the best day."
Ben

Makes notes of your child's comments and use them to journal.

Silhouette a large shape to give the page a focus.

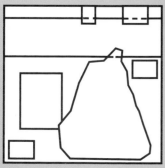

Jazz up the page using single and layered card stock rectangles.

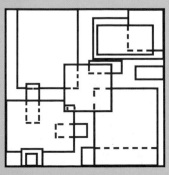

Turn vellum on point (to make a diamond) to soften part of the background.

trip to nebraska

make it fast using an old atlas or map. To soften the effect, place a vellum square on point over the background, allowing the corners of the map to show brilliantly.

materials

- photo
- 12-inch square of orange card stock
- 12×10½-inch rectangle from atlas or map
- 12-inch square of vellum
- 8×9-inch piece of textured turquoise paper
- white printer paper
- 2 daisy die cuts
- paper trimmer
- computer and printer
- tape
- glue stick

our trip to

NEBRASKA

Complement the travel theme with a map section from the highlighted area.

Print the headline on white paper, leaving room for a photo.

Glue colorful die cuts at the top and bottom of the page.

Secure vellum in the center, fold the corners to the back, and tape.

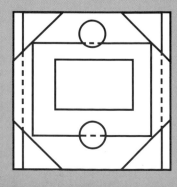

our day at the mall

make it fast using colorful paper circles and squares to back photos and increase contrast on the page. To crop circles in seconds use a circle cutter. A paper trimmer makes squares, rectangles, and strips in just a couple of quick slices.

materials

- photos
- 12-inch square of black card stock
- card stock in white, red, yellow, turquoise, and blue
- white paper
- conversation blurb stickers
- paper trimmer
- computer and printer
- circle cutter
- glue stick

Print the headline and subheads on white paper and cut them into strips.

Use a circle cutter to make circles in a jiffy.

Overlap a white card stock circle over the end of the headline box to make a unit.

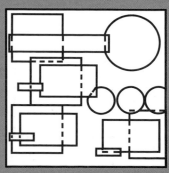

make it fast with a paper trimmer or purchased precut pieces of card stock. Choosing only two or three colors helps unify the pages. Punch out the headline letters and square accents.

materials

- photos
- two 12-inch squares of medium green card stock
- 12-inch squares of card stock in dark green and white
- 8½×11-inch rectangles of card stock in tan and light green
- scrap of black card stock
- alphabet die cut machine or die cut letters for headline
- square punch
- paper punch
- 3 black brads
- paper trimmer
- computer and printer
- glue stick

De Smet

South Dakota – June 10-11, 2002
The Real Little Town on the Prairie
Site of Laura Ingalls Wilder's books:
By The Shores of Silver Lake
The Long Winter
Little Town on the Prairie
These Happy Golden Years
The First Four Years

After touring the Black Hills, we headed toward De Smet, childhood home of Laura Ingalls Wilder. Bailey in particular is a great fan of the author, and it was a real thrill to visit another significant site mentioned in her books. It was interesting to compare this site to Rocky Ridge in Mansfield, Missouri, where we visited a few years ago.

We started our tour in the original Surveyors' House. We picked up a map which showed the 16 sites that could be visited in DeSmet. Bailey insisted that we see the sites in the order they were numbered on the map (not necessarily the most convenient route)! Grandpa patiently drove us around (and back and forth) to see and photograph all of the sites, and Bailey enlightened us with their significance.

Leave space at the top of the journal box for the headline.

Punch out squares from card stock and glue in pairs.

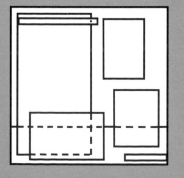

Adhere the same color of card stock strips across two pages.

In this book, the people of the town of DeSmet finds themselves snowbound for many, many months and with an extreme shortage of food. Almanzo, Laura's future husband, and Cap Garland, risk their lives to buy wheat to save the town from starving.

This is the first book which takes place in De Smet, where Laura would meet Almanzo and remain until after she married. We are reintroduced to some of Laura's family, which we had not seen since *Little House in the Big Woods.* De Smet changes from a railroad camp to a bustling frontier town.

Opposite page:
1. Original homestead site outside of De Smet
2. Some of the 5 original cottonwood trees planted by Charles Ingalls (Pa)
3. Memorial at homestead site

This page:
4. Big Slough, just across from the homestead site, mentioned in books
5. Statue of Father De Smet
6. Surveyors' House where the family lived upon moving to De Smet (1879-80)

Attach small card stock rectangles with brads.

Make a tag shape by clipping off two corners of a rectangle.

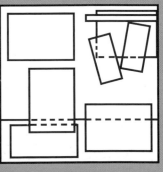

hawaii band trip

make it fast using mirror-image art elements available on page 185 and 187. The tree and wave designs coordinate with any sea theme. With the additions of the sun and floral motifs, all these pages need are photos!

materials
- photos
- two 12-inch squares of gold card stock
- 12-inch square of plum card stock
- scrap of pink card stock
- photocopy of art, page 185 and 187
- white alphabet stickers
- scissors
- paper trimmer
- permanent marking pens
- glue stick

Art in back of book!

see page 185 and 187

view from top of Diamondhead

PARADISE COVE

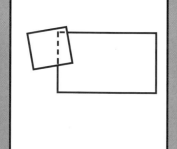

Layer the decorative frame, matted photo, and flower cutout.

Enlarge art of waves on page 185 to 110 percent to extend the width of the paper.

Color in white alphabet stickers to create a bold headline.

HAWAII BAND TRIP

Caitlyn · Taylor · Megan · Travis

top of Diamondhead

Make a
mirror-image copy
of the wave for the
right page.

Color in the
alphabet stickers to
coordinate with the
page colors.

Silhouette a flower
from the photo mat
for a corner accent.

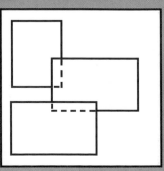

QUICK TIP

summer storm

make it fast by accenting the page with monochromatic squares and stripes. Tie two pages together by placing narrow horizontal stripes across the spread.

materials

- photos
- two 12-inch squares of navy blue card stock
- 12-inch squares of card stock in light and medium blue-gray
- scraps of navy blue card stock
- paper trimmer
- computer and printer
- date stamp
- glue stick

JUN 08 2003

After visiting South Dunes Beach, we decided the girls needed to get their swimming suits on so they could actually get in the ocean. After a quick change, we scampered down the path to "our beach" as we had already started to call it, just a short walking distance from our condo. Bailey and Mallory played in the shallow water while Jay and I waded and looked for shells. I loved the feel of sand, the salty spray, and the sounds of the waves and birds overhead. I was fascinated by the trees that face the beach. They are gnarled and contorted, as if they have been permanently shaped by the weather.

Balance the pages by placing square designs in opposite corners of spread.

Mat only the focal point photos.

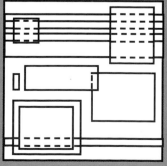

Cut a square diagonally to create two triangles.

While we were there, the wind started to pick up, making the water very choppy. Suddenly, the skies darkened and immense clouds began to form. I was surprised at how quickly the storm began to gather. We plucked the girls out of the water and ran for cover just before the rain came. We were told that these sudden storms are common on the island, but they don't usually last long.

Summer Storm

Place the title on the right-hand page for interest.

Stylize the background using monochromatic strips of card stock.

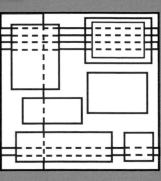

idaho snow

make it fast by featuring one color of solid card stock and the exclusive art elements from pages 189 and 191. These pages use lavender, but choose any color to complement your photos.

materials

- photos
- two 12-inch squares of lavender card stock
- card stock in red and white
- color photocopy of art, pages 189 and191
- alphabet stickers
- marking pens in white and black
- scissors
- paper trimmer
- glue stick

Art in back of book!

see pages 189 and 191

IDAHO

Dearest Friends
Ron and Juanita
Lil and Julian
Donnie and Nancy
and Lori

Position the photocopies of the animals to face into the pages.

Create a snowball out of white card stock, accenting with white marking pen lines.

Handwrite simple journaling: a subhead and a record of names.

QUICK TIP

Use decorative-edge scissors to cut quick zigzag borders.

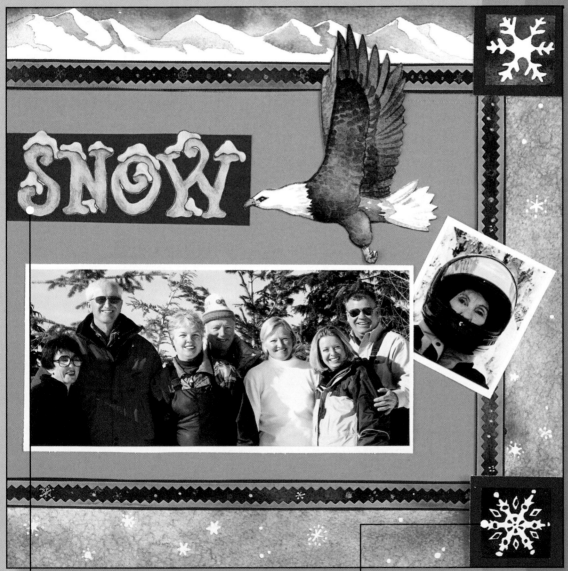

Apply alphabet stickers to contrasting card stock for the headline.

Use a different snowflake design in each corner.

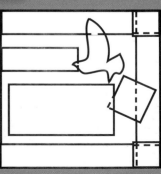

materials

- photos
- 8½×11-inch black card stock
- card stock in light blue, red, yellow, green, white, and purple
- photocopy of car patterns, page 153
- vellum postcard sticker
- fine-line black marking pen
- computer and printer; scissors
- paper trimmer
- glue stick

Patterns in back of book

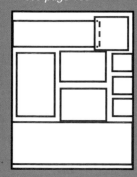

see page 153

on the road

make it fast by cropping photos to fit in a grid pattern. Choose a solid background paper that contrasts with the photos to eliminate the need for matting. The patterns for the car border are on page 153.

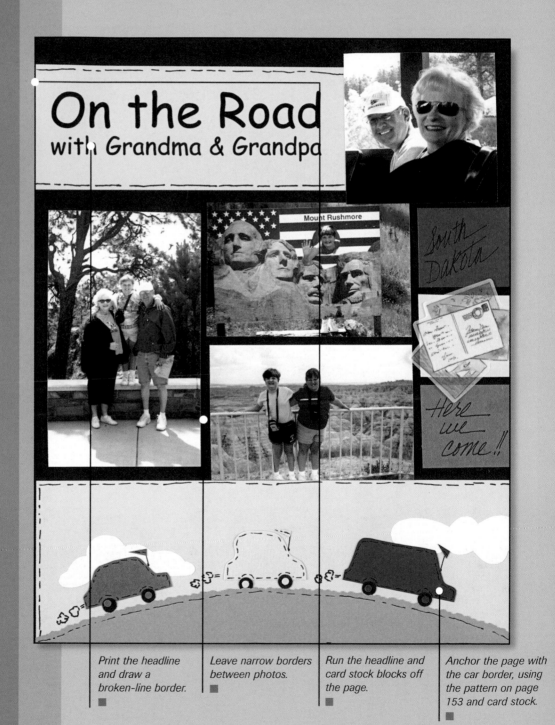

Print the headline and draw a broken-line border.

Leave narrow borders between photos.

Run the headline and card stock blocks off the page.

Anchor the page with the car border, using the pattern on page 153 and card stock.

shedd aquarium

make it fast using a travel brochure to accent the page and to remember details from a trip. Attach it to the page with a paper strip embellished with punched squares and string.

Shedd Aquarium

Chicago, Illinois | June, 2002

A real highlight of our trip to Chicago was spending time at the Shedd Aquarium. We loved the Caribbean Reef exhibit where we could watch divers feed the sea turtle and hear them discuss ocean life while diving. We met unusual creatures in the touch tank, observed delicate seahorses for the first time, and watched an amazing and educational dolphin show. Before the show,

one of the trainers asked Bailey to be her helper, which would have involved putting on wading boots and possibly getting a little bit wet by walking out into the pool area. We were disappointed (but not surprised) that she declined. Nevertheless, it was a great show, and we were thrilled to see these beautiful animals up close.

materials
- photos
- 12-inch square of black card stock
- 4¼×12-inch rectangle of white card stock
- card stock in royal and light blue
- brochure
- square black eyelets and eyelet tool
- black string
- square punch
- computer and printer
- paper trimmer
- glue stick
- rubber cement

Position the headline at the top of a two-column journal box.

Tape string ends on the back of the background card stock.

Glue punched squares along a paper strip and attach an eyelet at each end.

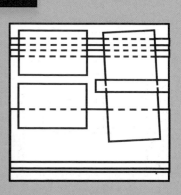

Let the Games Begin!

LET THE FUN BEGIN

Our Vacation at Last!

A Trip to Remember

Are we there yet?

gone fishin'

Ready...Set...Let's Go!

VACATIONS

ROCK

stop and smell the flowers

■ ■ ■ ■ ■

Planting flowers,

watching the

seasons change,

heading to the fair—

life is good!

Remember all of the

special times with

clever pages

bursting with fun.

preserving
memories

autumn

make it fast with blocks of textured card stock that provide interest and movement to an organized page. Mount the photos on the same color to simplify. For the background, cut two contrasting strips of card stock, placing the darker color on the bottom for weight.

materials

- photos
- 12-inch squares of textured card stock in burnt orange, olive, gold, and red
- blue textured card stock
- autumn die cut
- leaf punches
- black fine-line marking pen
- paper trimmer
- glue stick

Use a computer to print journaling on color card stock.

Choose a die cut with a white background to stand out from the color background.

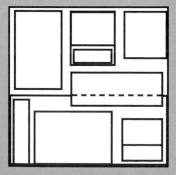

*Use a purchased
die cut to provide a
two-second headline.*

Autumn's in the Air

*Use a leaf punch to
make colorful die
cuts that relate to
the theme.*

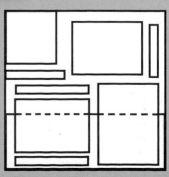

QUICK TIP

Make a simple photo spectacular by cutting it into equal horizontal or vertical strips.

materials

- photos
- 12-inch square of olive green card stock
- card stock in raspberry, light raspberry, and light olive
- olive vellum
- small metal floral plaque
- eyelets and eyelet tool
- computer and printer
- glue stick

backyard beauty

make it fast using rectangles. Crop the photos, cut or tear the papers, even choose a metal plaque embellishment—all rectangular. This lovely example combines 24 rectangles in harmonious, stunning fashion.

Place the torn-vellum headline over a row of photo strips.

Liven up the background with layered card stock strips.

Choose a mat color that coordinates with the pictured blooms.

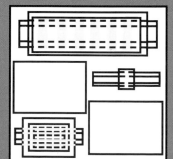

golf

watch a game, it's fun.
u play it, it's recreation.
u work at it, it's golf.
Bob Hope

make it fast by combining large photos and stickers on a solid card stock background. Choose three photos to tell the story and angle one for pizzazz. Fill in the blank areas with stickers and journaling.

Cover an unimportant part of a photo with a quotation or journaling.

I followed the guys out To the Pinewood Golf Course and snapped away! What great shots of Jared & John on the course!!!!!!!!

"If you watch a game, it's fun. If you play it, it's recreation. If you work at it, it's golf." *Bob Hope*

Golf

materials
- photos
- 12-inch square of green card stock
- card stock in white and light green
- golf stickers
- eyelets and eyelet tool
- paper trimmer
- glue stick

Angle a photo for flair. Mount the photo on white to contrast from the background.

Place a sticker on card stock, trim, and glue to an open area in the photograph.

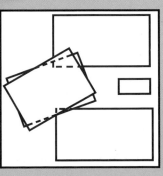

whatsa buckeye?

make it fast using enlarged photos. Pick a vertical shot to run the full length of the page. For accents enlarge a photo with elements that relate to the theme, such as the buckeyes at the page bottom.

Print a black background and reverse lettering on scrapbook paper.

materials

- 2 enlarged photos, one vertical and one to silhouette shapes
- 12-inch square of coordinating print scrapbook paper
- 8½×11-inch scrapbook paper to fit in printer
- tan paper
- scissors
- paper trimmer
- computer and printer
- glue stick

WHATSA

BUCKEYE???

buckeye (buk-'ĭ) American chestnut, hand picked by Anne Mae on a beautiful fall day for Mom to make her crafts

Silhouette elements from one of the enlargements.

Place the vertical photo left of center.

Use a dictionary-style definition to explain a theme.

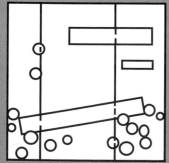

link to the past

make it fast by printing the subhead and journaling on the background paper. For variety, print at the bottom of the page, breaking the type into two columns. This leaves room for photos at the top.

QUICK TIP

Cut out a sign from a photo to create a headline.

A Link to the Past

In November, 2002, I attended a Girl Scout leader training session at Camp Juliette in Marshalltown. This was really fun for me because I have vivid memories of the weekends my childhood Girl Scout troop spent at what was then called Camp Juliette Low. With my mom and Louise Beattie as leaders, we stayed in the big, old house on the property, cooking in the expansive kitchen and sleeping in the spooky attic. It was there that I learned how to make French toast, scrambled eggs, and macramé belts and bracelets.

When I returned to Camp Juliette as a leader myself, it made me quite sad that the old house was long gone, but I found the spot back in the trees where it once stood and a few pictures of it in dusty, long-forgotten books. A new lodge serves today's Girl Scout troops. Our group had a good time cooking, playing games, and making crafts. This time, I learned how to make French toast casserole and a dump cake in a heavy, old Dutch oven in the big stone fireplace, things I will pass along to my own daughter...

materials

- photos
- 12-inch square of dark brown card stock
- card stock in light and medium brown
- leaf die cut
- eyelets and cyelet tool
- computer and printer
- brown chalk
- paper trimmer
- glue stick

Mount two of the photos on card stock and trim narrow borders.

Chalk the edges of the mat papers.

Group the silhouetted headline and the leaf die cut.

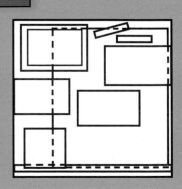

moving day

make it fast using photocopies of newspaper clippings. Combine them with present photos for a historical style.

Place stickers on cream card stock and chalk the edges for a vintage look.

materials
- photos
- photocopy of newspaper clipping
- 12-inch square of white card stock
- card stock in brown, black, dark olive, and cream
- alphabet, numeral, and embellishment stickers
- date stamp
- paper trimmer
- brown chalk
- glue stick

The old Simpson house was soon to get a new lease on life as the Johnston historical museum, but first it had to be moved to a new location near the Johnston Public Library. When Bailey read in the paper that moving day was coming, she asked if we could watch. So we drove up the street and watched while the old house was slowly moved from the old lot and down the street (1). After observing for awhile, we drove to the new location and waited with a few other neighbors until we could see it coming down the street (2), followed by the top of the barn (3). Finally, both came to rest safely at their new location (4). Bailey was keenly interested in the events of moving day. It is not every day that you see a house and barn traveling down the street!

JUN 2 4 2002

HISTORICAL SOCIETY ON THE MOVE — Buildings from a farmstead that was in rural Johnston for most of its history are being preserved for a local museum. They were moved on June 25, from their previous location in the city's developing area near N.W. 86th Street and N.W. 70th Avenue. The farm has been occupied over the years by the Bauman, Garlock and Simpson families. The Simpsons donated the buildings to the Johnston Historical Society, which plans to make them part of a local attraction. In this photo, the house is being trucked across 70th, with the barn trailing close behind. They were relocated to the new Johnston Commons area, just west of Merle Hay Road and Northglenn Drive, behind the Johnston Public Library.

Place alphabet stickers in a wavy fashion.

Angle a newspaper clipping for drama.

Align photos vertically on the right-hand side.

national guard

make it fast with minimal trimming and premade embellishments. This page combines a die-cut headline, an enlarged photo, tags, dimensional stickers, mesh, and theme-print paper to capture the effect.

Personalize a plain tag using alphabet and word stickers.

materials

- photo
- two 12-inch squares of coordinating scrapbook papers
- 6½×12-inch piece of black adhesive mesh
- diecut headline
- 2 metal tags on ball chain
- black alphabet and word stickers with clear background
- dimensional military-theme stickers
- date stamp
- black fine-line marking pen
- scissors
- glue stick

Create texture with a wide strip of mesh.
■

Overlay the headline in the center of the page
■

Handwrite journaling on the photo.
■

Trim top paper and align with the bottom right corner of the coordinating paper.

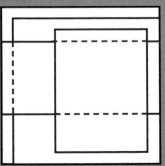

state fair

make it fast by highlighting an element from the photos for artistic embellishments. The tents in these photos are easily re-created from simple paper shapes.

materials

- photos
- two 12-inch squares of dark blue card stock
- 12-inch squares of card stock in green red, white, and yellow
- chile pepper sticker
- square punch
- computer and printer
- paper trimmer
- scissors
- glue stick

2003 Iowa State Fair
Chili Cook-Off

August, 2003   As told by Jay Petersma, Judge

queen sighting   good tasting   long deliberating

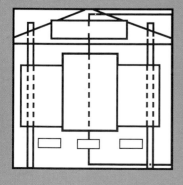

Print headline and journaling on one piece of paper and crop around blocks.

Embellish pages with punched squares, turning some on point.

QUICK TIP

August, 2003

200
Å

Use logos provided on a related website to accent a page.

I had the great fortune to be a judge for the 2003 International Chili Society's Iowa State Fair Chili Cook-Off. It was sponsored by Stockman's Inn, itself a fair institution. There were about 22 entries who cooked their special recipes down into some of the most delicious chili I've ever had. The chili had to be "Texas-style" - no beans allowed, and everything had to be cooked right there on site. All judging was anonymous, and the 12 judges didn't know who had made each batch as we tasted the fantastic creations. The one disappointment was that no one made a really hot chili, as I would have given it the number one spot almost automatically. After a morning of tasting, all of the entries began to become one big "chili blur." In the end, we had one plump judge's belly and three winners. Of those, I had selected only one but enjoyed the process enormously!

crowd watching

chili wafting

judge resting

Place paper rectangles on the inside edges to unify pages.

Leave most photos uncropped, matting only two.

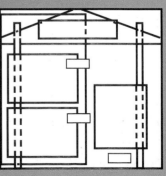

139

gardening

make it fast by dividing the page with wide horizontal and narrow vertical strips. This approach separates the pages into a grid, facilitating quick organization.

materials
- photos
- two 12-inch squares *each* of dark olive and light olive card stock
- two ¼×12-inch strips of plum card stock
- scraps of card stock in pink, mauve, plum, medium olive, and rust
- paper trimmer
- large and small flower punches
- large and small circle punches
- computer and printer
- glue stick
- glue dots

Punch flowers from card stock and adhere to background with glue dots.

Adhere flower centers with glue stick.

Cut freehand stems and leaves.

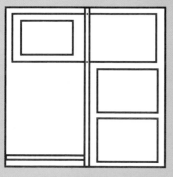

| my perennial canvas | spring - summer, 2002 |

After we removed the bushes around our patio, I had the opportunity to create a perennial garden. I knew from past mistakes that I needed to amend the soil, and Aunt Carole offered to give me soil from her farm in Carlisle. Mom and Dad brought it in late spring, and we worked it into a low mounded bed. I began work on designing the bed, determined that this time I would have success. I chose perennials that I love and paid attention to color (mostly purple) and bloom times. Some of the perennials (such as the coneflower and monarda) came from Grandma Gladys' garden. Grandma Weaver gave Bailey and me each a rose bush which we planted at the ends of the bed. I carefully labeled all the new plants (as shown in the first photo). To my delight, my garden flowers lived and bloomed profusely (as shown in the photos taken in July, 2002). As I write this in February, 2004, my little garden has grown for two summers. Some plants ended up a bit larger than I intended, others haven't done as well as I had hoped, and still others have succumbed to the bunnies, but overall the garden has provided vibrant color, flowers to cut and bring inside, and a new canvas on which to paint.

is the art that uses
flowers and plants
as *paint,*
and the soil and sky
as *canvas.*

Balance the headline block with journal blocks.

Devote each grid unit to photos, punched flowers, or journaling.

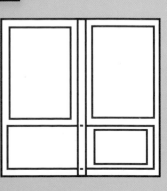

For a polished look, glue baby rickrack along a seam where two papers meet.

materials

- photos
- 12×4-inch piece of lime green card stock
- 12×9-inch piece of pink polka-dot paper
- cardstock in pink, white, and lime green
- scrap of pink striped paper
- white baby rickrack
- large pink pom-pom
- pink flocking, such as Fun Flock
- alphabet stamps
- pink ink pad
- scissors
- paper trimmer
- glue stick
- thick white crafts glue

cotton candy days

make it fast by mixing large photos and minimal embellishment. Here four photos nearly fill the page, leaving just enough room for a stamped headline and cotton candy accents.

COTTON CANDY DAYS

The Anderson's borrowed a cotton candy machine and made cotton candy for all the neighborhood kids!

Dot green paper with crafts glue and sprinkle with flocking.

Cut a pom-pom in half to make cotton candy. Roll a 1×2-inch strip of paper for the handle.

Overlap the top paper strip 1 inch, gluing to secure the papers.

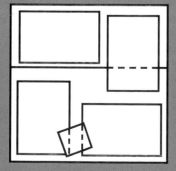

blossoming music

make it fast with rubber-stamped embellishments. You can create an endless array of designs by changing the ink colors to complement your theme.

Blossoming through

MUSIC

Pace Festival
April, 2002

You can see from these photos that Bailey and her piano partner, Brynn Schor, had a great time at this year's Pace Festival. Their teacher, Mrs. Canine, uses the Pace method in her teaching, which encompasses music theory and composition in addition to traditional piano performance. Each year or so, the local teachers who use the Pace method have a clinic or festival for students to learn and play in ensembles. This event focused on duets, and a teacher from out of state came to work with the students. Although much more difficult than traditional methods, we feel that Bailey has really blossomed in terms of her music knowledge by being exposed to this way of teaching.

materials
- photos
- 12-inch square of white card stock
- 12-inch square of royal blue card stock
- 12-inch square of blue print paper
- scraps of card stock in black and white
- flower rubber stamp
- ink pads in blue, black, and yellow
- black brads
- ¾-inch black alphabet stickers
- ribbon momento
- scissors
- small paper punch
- paper trimmer
- computer and printer
- glue stick
- adhesive spacers, such as Pop Dots

Use brads or black card stock triangles in each corner.

Mat photos simply using black and white card stock.

Apply alphabet stickers on scrapbook paper and tear the edges.

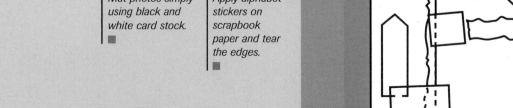

vember, 2003
our old house, we had a
nt yard. It shed long, sp
would poke right thr
enough, there are
se also. They

*Print journaling on light
color 8½×11-inch paper;
overlap with card stock.*

ode to the pods

make it fast with a color-blocked card stock background. Choose three or four colors that coordinate with your photos and cut the card stock into squares and rectangles. For a more textural look tear the edges.

materials

- photos
- 12-inch square of dark brown card stock
- card stock scraps to coordinate with photos
- 8½×11-inch piece of light color paper
- leaf die cut
- brads
- paper punch
- paper trimmer
- computer and printer
- glue stick

ODE TO THE PODS

November, 2003
In our old house, we had a gigantic locust tree in the front yard. It shed long, spiky thorns, so sharp that they would poke right through the sole of your shoe. Sure enough, there are locust trees the backyard of this house also. They don't have thorns, but they are prolific pod-producers, and we watch with trepidation each summer as the pods are formed. Some years are worse than others, and this year was particularly bad (bad enough for Jay to write this poem). The pods dropped over a period of several days, then the wind picked them up and blew them everywhere, including into the neighboring yards. Jan's parents came to help rake and hauled away an entire dump truck full. Jan continues to believe there is surely some way to use the pods for crafting...

By Jay Petersma
Pods are falling all around,
See them dropping to the ground.
They're ugly, rattley, crusty brown...
I just wish they'd all fall down!

The pods are down!
We rake a lot!
We love to gather them up....NOT!

Adhere a die cut to a small piece of card stock.

Plan journaling in blocks at the top and bottom of the page. Use an ink color complementary to the card stock.

Place some blocks to run to the edge of the page.

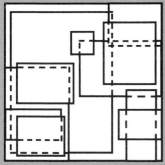

quotable quotes

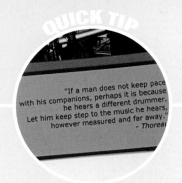

When you want fast journaling ideas, incorporate quotes into your pages. Several books and online sources are available. Here are some great comments to get you started.

kids

Children are the sum of what mothers contribute to their lives.

—*Unknown*

In raising my children, I have lost my mind but found my soul.

—*Lisa T. Shepherd*

Good parents give their children roots and wings. Roots to know where home is, wings to fly away and exercise what's been taught them.

—*Jonas Salk*

All kids need is a little help, a little hope and somebody who believes in them.

—*Earvin "Magic" Johnson*

All the birds in the sky, all the fish in the sea, will never explain what you mean to me.

—*Courtney Maddox*

If you can give your son or daughter only one gift, let it be enthusiasm.

—*Bruce Barton*

family

Family isn't about whose blood you have. It's about who you care about.

—*Trey Parker and Matt Stone*

Men are what their mothers made them.

—*Ralph Waldo Emerson*

Acting is just a way of making a living; the family is life.

—*Denzel Washington*

Bringing up a family should be an adventure, not an anxious discipline in which everybody is constantly graded for performance.

—*Milton R. Saperstein*

The most important thing a father can do for his children is to love their mother.

—*Theodore M. Hesburgh*

Everything I am or ever hope to be, I owe to my angel mother.

—*Abraham Lincoln*

travel

Stop worrying about the potholes in the road and enjoy the journey.

—*Babs Hoffman*

The world is a book, and those who do not travel read only a page.

—*Augustine (354-430)*

I am one of those who never knows the direction of my journey until I have almost arrived.

—*Anna Louise Strong*

The rewards of the journey far outweigh the risk of leaving the harbor.

—*Unknown*

A journey of a thousand miles begins with a single step.

—*Confucius*

I love to travel, but hate to arrive.

—*Albert Einstein*

If you actually look like your passport photo, you aren't well enough to travel.

—*Sir Vivian Fuchs*

miscellaneous

One loyal friend is better than ten thousand family members.

—*Unknown*

The most important trip you may take in life is meeting people halfway.

—*Henry Boye*

What do you call people who are afraid of Santa Claus? Claustrophobic.

—*Unknown*

Everything is funny as long as it is happening to somebody else.

—*Will Rogers*

If you love something, set it free; if it comes backs it's yours, if it doesn't, it never was.

—*Richard Bach*

What we love to do we find time to do.

—*John L. Spalding*

The torch of love is lit in the kitchen.

—*French proverb*

The Good Ol' Days

Girls just wanna have fun!

Boys just wanna have fun!

family   friends

GROOVY!

Life is good!

glossary

Acid-free

Acid is used in paper manufacturing to break apart the wood fibers and the lignin that holds them together. If acid remains in the materials used for photo albums, the acid can react chemically with photographs and cause their deterioration. Acid-free products have a pH factor of 7.0 or above. It's imperative that all materials (glue, pens, papers, etc.) used in memory albums or scrapbooks be acid-free.

Acid migration

Acid migration is the transfer of acidity from one item to another through physical contact or acidic vapors. If a newspaper clipping is put into an album, the area it touches will eventually turn yellow or brown. A deacidification pH factor spray can be used on acidic papers, or they can be photocopied onto acid-free papers.

Adhesive

Scrapbooking adhesives include glue sticks, double-sided tape, spray adhesive, thick white crafts glue, mounting tabs, and other products. Read the labels to determine the best adhesive for the intended use.

Archival quality

Archival quality is a term used to indicate materials that have undergone laboratory analysis to determine that their acidic and buffered contents are within safe levels.

Borders

Borders are precut strips of patterned or solid paper used to add accent strips to a scrapbook page.

Brads

Small metal embellishments that are secured to paper by poking their prongs through the paper and bending the prongs outward from one another.

Buffered paper

During manufacture, a buffering agent, such as calcium carbonate or magnesium bicarbonate, can be added to paper to neutralize acid contaminant. Such papers have a pH of 8.5.

Card stock

Often used for the base or background of a page, card stock is a heavy paper with a smooth surface.

Corner rounder

Used like a paper punch, this tool rounds the corners of a photograph or paper.

Crafts knife

This tool has a replaceable small blade for cutting paper and other materials.

Cropping

Cutting or trimming a photo to keep only the most important parts of the image is called cropping.

Decorative-edge scissors

Available in a wide assortment of cutting blades, these scissors cut wavy, scalloped, zigzagged, or other decorative edges in paper and other thin materials.

Die cut

This is a paper embellishment in which the background has been cut away. Die cuts come in hundreds of shapes and sizes.

Eyelets

Small metal embellishments have an open circular center. When set, eyelets can attach thin items (such as paper or fabric) or provide a hole for lacing.

Glossy

A smooth, shiny appearance or finish is referred to as glossy.

Glue stick

A glue stick is a solid stick-type glue that is applied by rubbing.

Journaling

Journaling refers to text on a scrapbook page that provides details about the photographs. Journaling can be done in your own handwriting, with adhesive letters, rub-ons, stencils, or it can be computer generated.

Lignin

Lignin is the material that holds wood fibers together as a tree grows. If lignin remains in the final paper (as with newsprint), it becomes yellow and brittle over time. Most papers other than newsprint are lignin-free.

Mat

Mats are varying weights of paper used to frame photographs using single or multiple layers.

Matte

A dull surface or finish, not shiny or glossy, is considered matte.

Opaque

Colors that are dense and cannot be seen through are opaque.

Paper punch

This handheld tool punches out circles, hearts, diamonds, and other shapes in stencil form.

Paper trimmer

A paper-cutting tool with a surface for holding the paper and a sharp blade that cuts the paper in a straight line.

pH factor

The pH factor refers to the acidity of a paper. The pH scale, a standard for measurement of acidity and alkalinity, runs from 0 to 14, each number representing a ten-fold increase; neutral is 7. Acid-free products have a pH factor of 7 or above. Special pH-tester pens are available to determine the acidity or alkalinity of products.

Photo-safe

Photo-safe is a term similar to archival quality but more specific to materials used with photographs. Acid-free is the determining factor for a product to be labeled photo-safe.

Protective sleeves

Made of plastic to slip over a finished album page, sleeves can be side-loading or top-loading and fit $8\frac{1}{2}\times11$-inch or 12-inch-square pages. Choose only acid-free sleeves. Polypropylene (vinyl), commonly available for office use and is not archival quality.

Rubber stamping

Designs are etched into a rubber mat that is applied to a wood block. This rubber design is stamped onto an ink pad to transfer the design to paper or other surfaces.

Scrapbooking papers

Scrapbooking papers are usually 12-inch squares or $8\frac{1}{2}\times11$-inch rectangles. These include solids, patterns, textures, and vellum.

Stencil

Made from heavy paper or plastic, a stencil is laid flat on a surface. Paint or other medium is applied through the openings of the design to transfer it.

Stickers

Available in plastic, paper, vinyl, fabric, and other materials, stickers can be peeled from a backing paper and pressed into place.

Tracing paper

A sheer sheet of paper that can be seen through, it is usually used to trace a pattern.

Vellum

Available in white, colors, and patterns, this translucent paper has a frosted appearance.

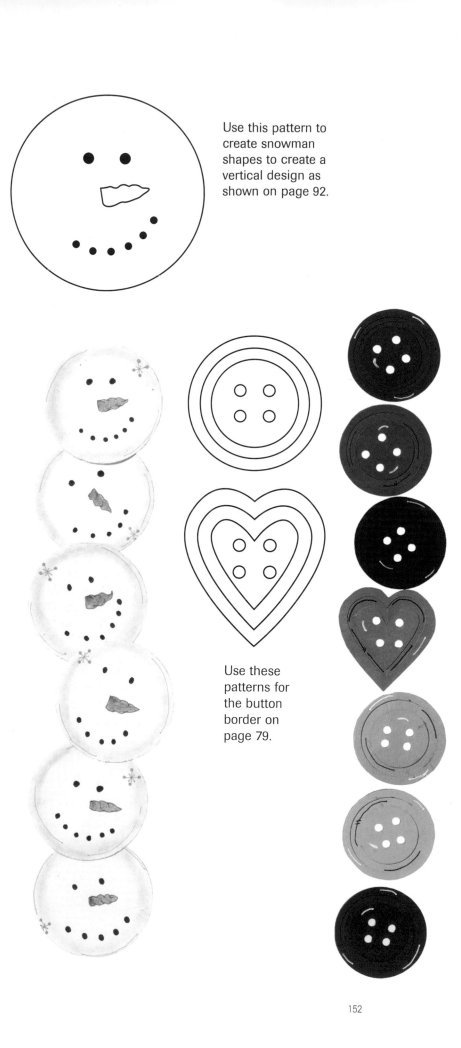

Use this pattern to create snowman shapes to create a vertical design as shown on page 92.

Use these patterns to make a border as shown on page 87. To fit a 12-inch page, splice two strips together.

Use these patterns for the button border on page 79.

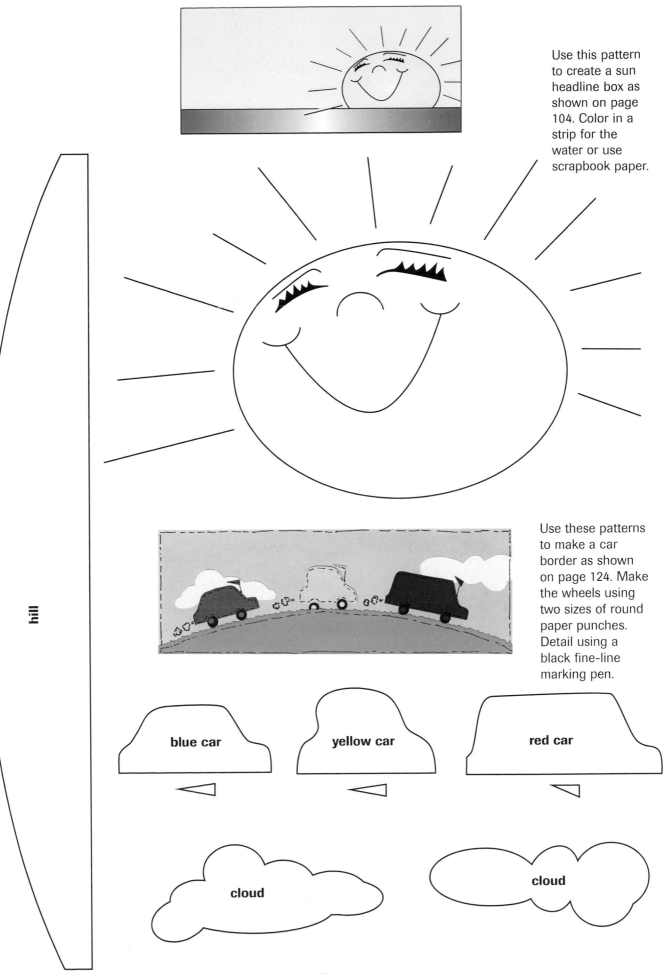

Use this pattern to create a sun headline box as shown on page 104. Color in a strip for the water or use scrapbook paper.

Use these patterns to make a car border as shown on page 124. Make the wheels using two sizes of round paper punches. Detail using a black fine-line marking pen.

hill

blue car

yellow car

red car

cloud

cloud

Tag Patterns

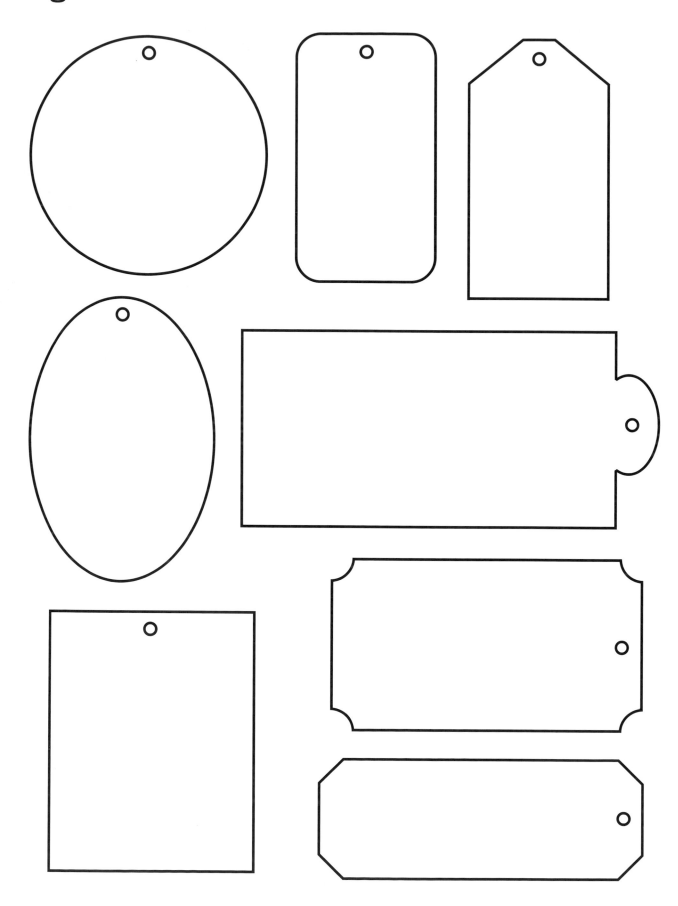

sources

Adhesives
Aleenes
duncancrafts.com

Centis
Centis Consumer Products
Division
888/236-8476

Elmer's Glue Stick
800/848-9400
elmers.com
comments@elmers.com

Suze Weinberg Design
Studio
732/761-2400
732/761-2410 (fax)
Suzenj@aol.com

Tombow USA
800/835-3232
tombowusa.com

Brads
Magic Scraps
972/238-1838
magicscraps.com

Buttons
Le Bouton Buttons
Blumenthal Lansing Co.
563/538-4211
563/538-4243 (fax)
sales@buttonsplus.com

Die Cuts
Cock A Doodle
800/262-9727
cockadoodle.com

Deluxe Cuts
480/497-9005
707/922-2175 (fax)
deluxecuts.com

Fresh Cuts
Rebecca Sower
EK Success Ltd.
eksuccess.co

Griff's Shortcuts
989/894-5916
griffs-shortcuts.com

Little Extras
361/814-9191
littleextrasdiecuts.com

Stamping Station
801/444-3838
stampingstation.com

Eyelets
Persnippity
801/523-3338
persnippity.com

Fiber
Cut-It-Up
530/389-2233
cut-it-up.com

Foam Squares
Therm O Web
800/323-0799

**Opaque Writers/
Waterproof Markers**
EK Success Ltd.
eksuccess.com
(Wholesale only. Available at
most crafts stores.)

Protective Sleeves
Westrim Crafts
888/727-2727

**Rub-On Lettering
and Motifs**
Chartpak, Inc.
800/628-1910
800/762-7918 (fax)
chartpak.com

The Paper Patch
www.paperpatch.com
(Wholesale only. Available at
most crafts stores.)

Scrapbook Borders
scrapbookborders.com

Rubber Stamps/Ink Pads
Art Impressions
800/393-2014
artimpressions.com

Stampin' Up!
801/601-5400
stampinup.com

**Scissors, Punches &
Rounders**
Creative Memories
800/341-5275
creativememories.com

Fiskars Scissors
608/259-1649
fiskars.com

Emagination Crafts, Inc.
866/238-9770
service@
emaginationcraftsinc.com

EK Success Ltd.
eksuccess.com
(Wholesale only. Available at
most crafts stores.)

Scrapbook Papers
All My Memories
888/553-1998

Anna Griffin
404/817-8170 (phone)
404/817-0590 (fax)
annagriffin.com

Art Accents
360/733-8989
artaccents.net

Bazzill Basics Paper
480/558-8557
bazzillbasics.com

Colorbök
800/366-4660
colorbok.com

Daisy D's Paper Co.
801/447-8955
daisydspaper.com

DMD, Inc.
800/805-9890

Doodlebug
801/966-9952

amily Archives
88/622-6556
eritagescrapbooks.com

rances Meyer, Inc.
00/372-6237
ancesmeyer.com

ot Off The Press, Inc.
00/227-9595
aperpizazz.com

aren Foster Design, Inc.
arenfosterdesign.com

Making Memories
00/286-5263
makingmemories.com

Memories Forever
Westrim Crafts
00/727-2727
vestrimcrafts.com

he Paper Loft
66/254-1961 (toll free)
aperloft.com
Wholesale only. Available at
ost crafts stores.)

ixie Press
88/834-2883
ixiepress.com

laid Enterprises, Inc.
00/842-4197
laidonline.com

rovo Craft
rovocraft.com
Wholesale only. Available at
ost crafts stores.)

andylion
00/387-4215
05/475-0523 (International)
andylion.com

crap-ease What's New, Ltd.
00/272-3874
80/832-2928 (fax)
vhatsnewltd.com

Sweetwater
14711 Road 15
Fort Morgan, CO 80701
970/867-4428

Two Busy Moms
800/272-4794
TwoBusyMoms.com

Westrim Crafts
800/727-2727

Wübie Prints
wubieprints.com
(Wholesale only. Available at
most crafts stores.)

Stickers
Canson
800/628-9283
canson-us.com

The Gifted Line
John Grossman, Inc.
310/390-9900

Highsmith
800/558-3899
highsmith.com

K & Co.
816/389-4150
KandCompany.com

me & my BIG ideas
949/589-4607
meandmybigideas.com

Mrs. Grossman's Paper Co.
800/429-4549
mrsgrossmans.com

Once Upon A Scribble
702/896-2181
onceuponascribble.com

Paper Punch
800/397-2737

Paper House Productions
800/255-7316
paperhouseproductions.com

SRM Press
800/323-9589
srmpress.com
(Wholesale only. Available at
most crafts stores.)

Stickopotamus
P.O. Box 1047
Clifton, NJ 07014-1047
973/594-0540 (fax)
stickopotamus.com

Wire Mesh
ScrapYard 329
775/829-1118
scrapyard329.com

index

Several projects in
this book use
exclusive papers,
frames, and
embellishments—all
available on pages
161–191 for you to
photocopy and use
in your scrapbook.

artwork for
your pages

puppy

LOVE

BELOVED

best friend

faithful

Loyal companion

Emma & Honey

used on page 85

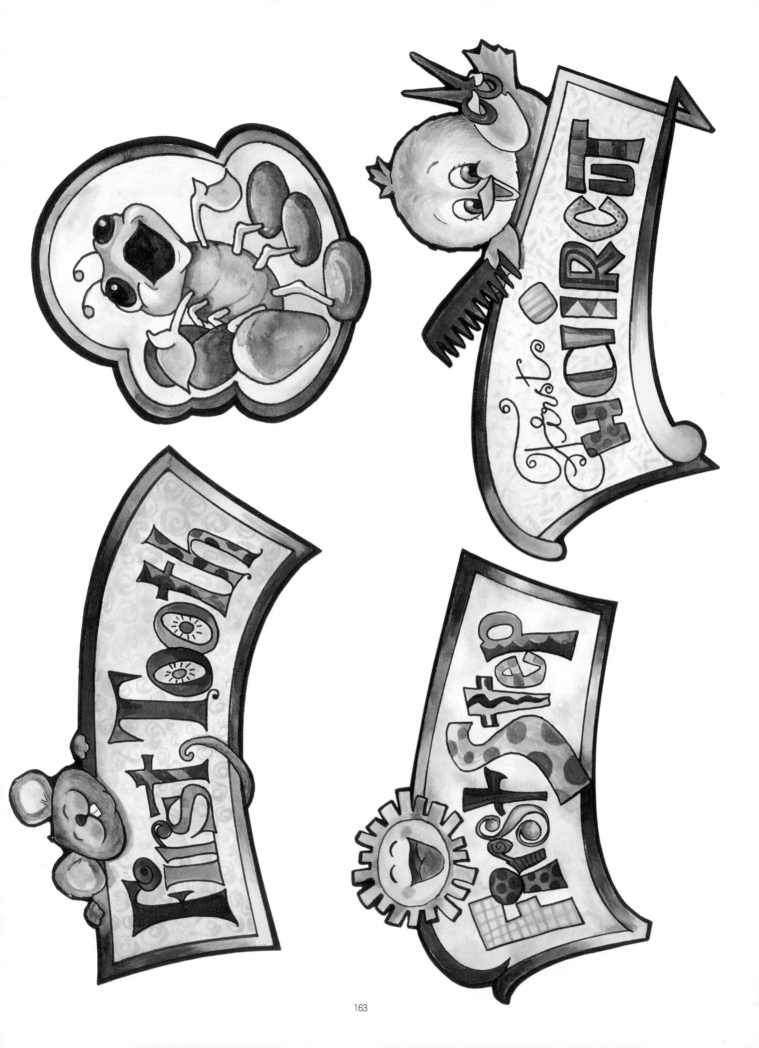

First Tooth and First Step

used on pages 50–51

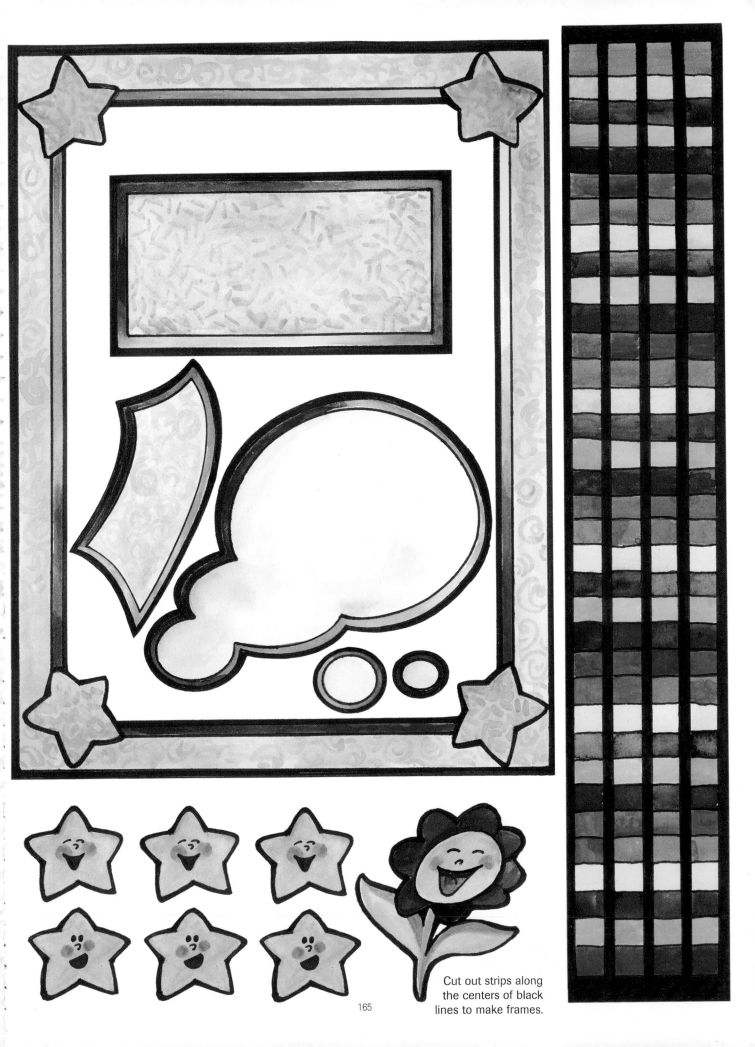

Cut out strips along
the centers of black
lines to make frames.

165

First Tooth and First Step

used on pages 50–51

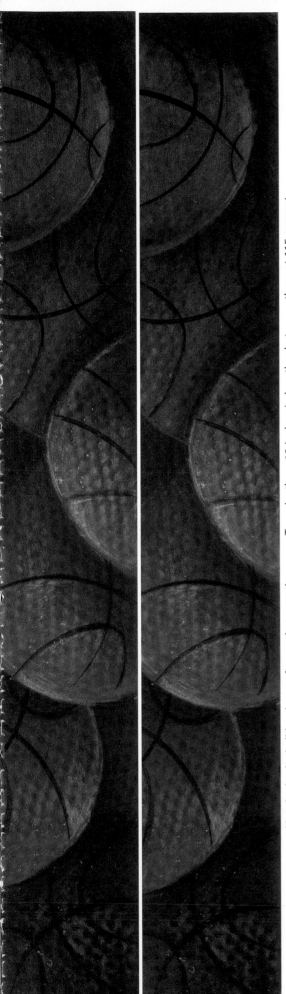

Use the basketball borders to frame photos or the page. To make them 12 inches in length, photocopy them at 115 percent.

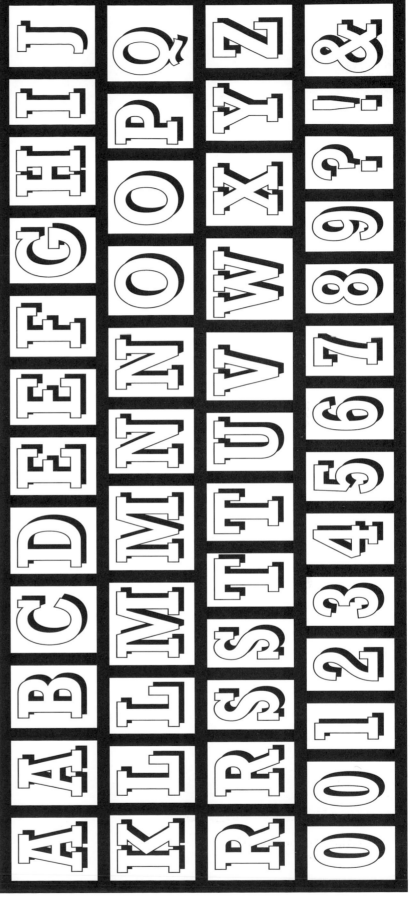

Use markers to color in the letters and numbers to suit your neecs.

Sep Rams and Two Home Runs

used on pages 66–67 and 71

Trim baseball around the outline. Write in your own all-star's signature.

Color in your own scoreboard headline using a bright color marker for words and using a black marker to fill in the rest, as shown on page 66.

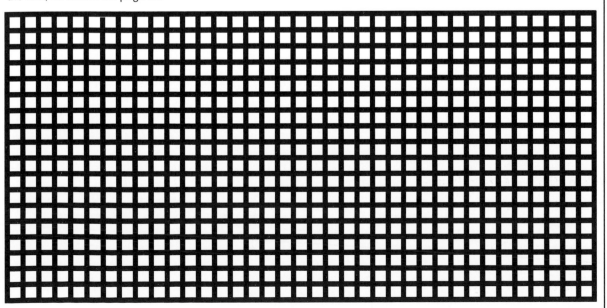

Sep Rams and Two Home Runs

used on pages 66–67 and 71

Visit with Santa

used on page 75

Cut out frame in the green border area. Trim border strips the same way.

Day in the Field

used on page 88

Grampa's Lake

used on page 91

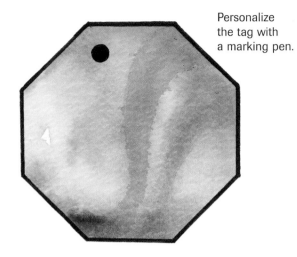

Personalize the tag with a marking pen.

Emma & Honey tag

used on page 85

My Cat

used on page 94

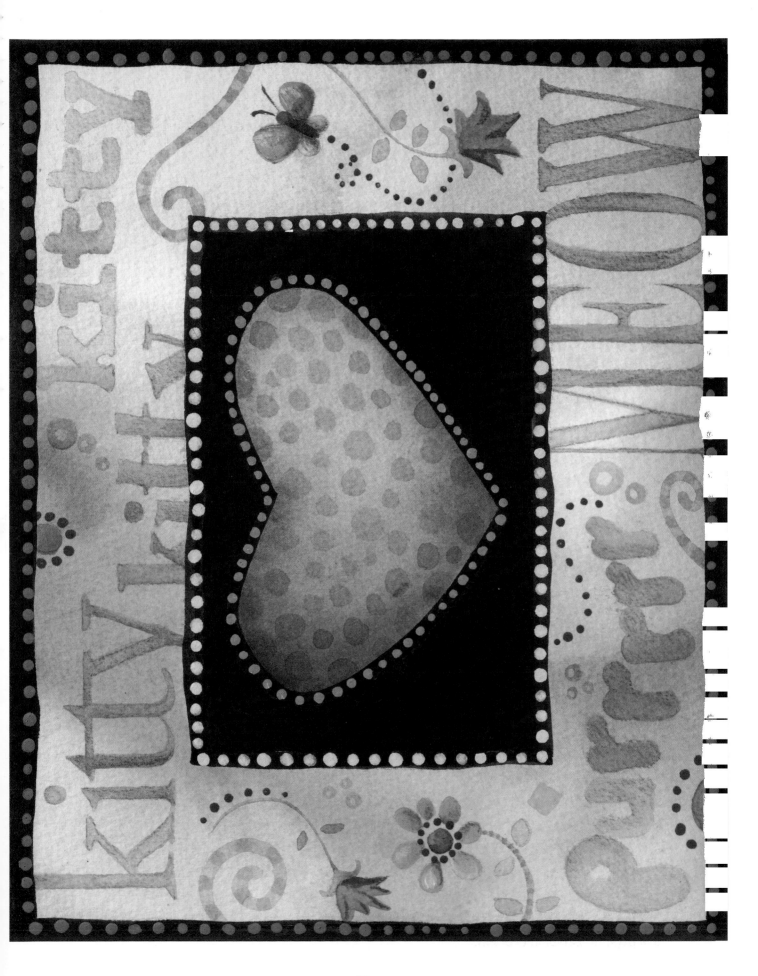

My Cat

used on page 94

Cat Sitter

used on page 95

Christmas with Sam

used on pages 96–97

To have the wave span 12 inches, photocopy the art at 110 percent. For a facing page, photocopy once using a mirror setting.

Use the floral border to frame a photo or to write a journal box.

Hawaii Band Trip

used on pages 118–119

Photocopy the tree once on regular setting and once on a mirror-image setting to have two facing palm trees.

Hawaii Band Trip

used on pages 118-119

Idaho Snow

used on pages 122–123

Idaho Snow

used on pages 122–123